SpringerBriefs in Offending Populations & Correctional Psychotherapy

Series Editor
Karla Sapp, Midway, GA, USA

SpringerBriefs in Offending Populations & Correctional Psychotherapy is a series of compact, high-quality volumes dealing with all aspects of the American carceral system and offender populations, from identifying systemic issues of the prison system to addressing services needed to support offender mental health.
Featuring concise titles between 50-125 pages, the cross-disciplinary series incorporates research and policy suggestions spanning mental health, criminal justice, and more, including topics such as correctional psychology and counseling, transformative and restorative justice, recidivism and rehabilitation, advocacy and public policy issues, and dismantling prison pipelines.
SpringerBriefs in Offending Populations & Correctional Psychotherapy will be of interest to a broad range of researchers and practitioners working in offender and prison research and in related academic fields such as Psychology, Counseling, Criminology, Criminal Justice, and Law.

Karla Sapp

Understanding Offending Populations and the Power of Correctional Psychotherapy

Unlocking Insights

Springer

Karla Sapp
Founder and Principal Licensed Psychotherapist
Project H.O.P.E. of Coastal Georgia, Inc
Midway, GA, USA

ISSN 2731-8966 ISSN 2731-8974 (electronic)
SpringerBriefs in Offending Populations & Correctional Psychotherapy
ISBN 978-3-031-45885-9 ISBN 978-3-031-45886-6 (eBook)
https://doi.org/10.1007/978-3-031-45886-6

This Springer imprint is published by the registered company Springer Nature Switzerland AG
The registered company address is: Gewerbestrasse 11, 6330 Cham, Switzerland

Preface

Understanding and addressing the complexities of offending populations is a significant challenge faced by the field of correctional psychology. In our quest to promote rehabilitation and reduce recidivism rates, it is crucial to delve deep into the minds and experiences of those who have engaged in criminal behavior. This book, *Understanding Offending Populations and the Power of Correctional Psychotherapy: Unlocking Insights*, aims to provide a comprehensive exploration of the factors that contribute to criminality, as well as the potential of correctional psychotherapy to unlock transformative insights and facilitate positive change.

Through the lens of empirical research, theoretical frameworks, and case studies, this book delves into the multifaceted aspects of offending populations, examining their psychological complexities and the environmental forces at play. By gaining a holistic understanding of these factors, we can better comprehend the underlying motivations and triggers behind criminal behavior. Moreover, this book sheds light on the power of correctional psychotherapy as an essential tool in promoting rehabilitation and healing. By utilizing evidence-based practices and therapeutic interventions, correctional psychologists and practitioners can help individuals navigate the underlying issues that contribute to their involvement in criminal activities.

The insights shared in this book are the result of years of research, practical experience, and collaboration between professionals in the field. It is my hope that this compilation of knowledge will provide readers with a deeper understanding of offending populations and the potential for correctional psychotherapy to bring about meaningful change. The journey toward comprehending and addressing the complexities of offending populations is an ongoing one, and it requires a multidisciplinary approach. By bringing together the fields of psychology, criminology, sociology, and more, it is my hope to facilitate a comprehensive understanding that can inform both policy-making and individual therapeutic endeavors.

I invite you, the reader, to embark on this journey with us, as we explore the intricacies of offending populations and unlock the transformative power of correctional psychotherapy. Together, we can work toward a more compassionate and effective approach to reducing recidivism and creating lasting positive change.

Midway, GA, USA Karla Sapp

Acknowledgments

I would like to express my deepest gratitude to all those who have contributed to the creation of *Understanding Offending Populations and the Power of Correctional Psychotherapy: Unlocking Insights*.

First and foremost, I extend my sincere appreciation to the individuals within the criminal justice system who have shared their invaluable experiences, perspectives, and knowledge. Their willingness to open up and offer insights into the complexities of offending behavior has been instrumental in shaping the content of this book.

I am immensely grateful to the numerous researchers and experts in the fields of criminology, psychology, and correctional psychotherapy whose work has provided the foundation for this book. Their groundbreaking research, innovative theories, and evidence-based practices have guided and informed the discussions throughout the chapters.

I owe a profound debt of gratitude to the clinicians, therapists, and mental health professionals who work tirelessly within correctional settings. Their dedication, compassion, and unwavering commitment to supporting offender rehabilitation have been a true inspiration. I am humbled by their resilience, resourcefulness, and the transformative impact they make in the lives of individuals under their care.

I would also like to acknowledge the support and encouragement of my colleagues and peers, who have provided valuable insights and feedback throughout the writing process. Your guidance and collaboration have been instrumental in shaping this book and enhancing its overall quality.

My heartfelt thanks go to the editorial and publishing team for their expertise, professionalism, and continuous support in bringing this book to life. Your meticulous attention to detail and unwavering belief in the importance of disseminating knowledge in this field have been truly commendable.

Finally, I am eternally grateful to my family, friends, and loved ones for their unwavering support, understanding, and encouragement throughout this endeavor. Your belief in me and your unwavering encouragement have been the cornerstone of my journey.

To all those mentioned and the countless others who have in some way contributed to this book, I offer my sincerest gratitude. It is with great pleasure and gratitude that I present *Understanding Offending Populations and the Power of Correctional Psychotherapy: Unlocking Insights* to the readers, hoping it will inspire meaningful dialogue, innovative practices, and positive change in the field of offender rehabilitation.

Contents

About the Author

Karla Sapp is a highly skilled and experienced practitioner who adeptly bridges the worlds of counseling, psychology, criminal justice, and corrections. With an EdD in Counseling Psychology, MA in Professional Counseling, and BS in Criminal Justice, as well as over a decade of hands-on experience working within the justice system, she has made significant contributions to the field. Dr. Karla's extensive experience working with diverse populations, including drug court participants and incarcerated individuals, provides her with valuable insights into the challenges and complexities faced by these individuals. This firsthand experience enables her to develop a deep understanding of their unique circumstances and tailor therapeutic interventions accordingly. She is currently a Licensed Professional Counselor in the state of Georgia and Licensed Mental Health Counselor in the state of Florida. She also holds the following credentials: Nationally Certified Counselor (NCC), Certified Clinical Mental Health Counselor (CCMHC), and Approved Clinical Supervisor (ACS).

Chapter 1
Introduction: Understanding Offending Populations and the Power of Correctional Psychotherapy—Unlocking Insights

In the realm of criminal justice and rehabilitation, understanding the intricacies of offending populations is essential for formulating effective interventions and promoting successful reintegration into society. To effectively address the needs of offending populations, a thorough understanding of their characteristics is crucial. Research by Andrews and Bonta (2010) suggests that certain risk factors, such as a history of childhood trauma, substance abuse, and antisocial attitudes, contribute to criminal behavior. By uncovering these underlying factors, we can gain insights into the motivations and patterns of offending, allowing for targeted and tailored interventions.

In the modern landscape of criminal justice, several issues warrant attention. For instance, the overrepresentation of certain groups, such as individuals with mental health disorders or those from marginalized communities, demands a closer examination of the systemic factors that contribute to their involvement in the criminal justice system (Barnao et al., 2017). Additionally, the need to address the specific needs of female offenders and juveniles underscores the importance of tailoring correctional psychotherapy interventions to diverse populations (Corrado & Roesch, 2017). By exploring these contemporary issues, practical insights and strategies could be offered to practitioners, researchers, and policymakers working in the field of offender rehabilitation.

Correctional psychotherapy has a rich historical background, evolving alongside shifts in societal attitudes toward offender rehabilitation. As stated by Latessa (2012), the early focus on punishment and retribution gradually gave way to a more rehabilitative approach, emphasizing the importance of addressing the psychological and behavioral aspects of criminal behavior. By tracing the development of correctional psychotherapy, we gain a deeper appreciation for the roots of this transformative approach and its potential impact on offender rehabilitation.

Central to the discussion of correctional psychotherapy is the goal of offender rehabilitation. The successful reintegration of offenders into society is a complex

K. Sapp, *Understanding Offending Populations and the Power of Correctional Psychotherapy*, SpringerBriefs in Offending Populations & Correctional Psychotherapy, https://doi.org/10.1007/978-3-031-45886-6_1

process that requires comprehensive support and evidence-based interventions. According to Palmer et al. (2017), effective rehabilitation programs not only address criminogenic needs and promote prosocial behaviors but also provide resources for education, employment, and social support. As such, developing a book emphasizing the importance of offender rehabilitation as a contemporary issue and exploring the role of correctional psychotherapy in achieving positive outcomes have become necessary.

Understanding Offending Population and the Power of Correctional Psychotherapy: A Case Study of Michael

Understanding the diverse characteristics and underlying factors that drive criminal behavior is essential for developing effective interventions within the correctional system. This case study examines the story of Michael, shedding light on the significance of understanding offender populations and the crucial role of correctional psychotherapy in promoting positive change.

Case Study:

Michael, a 42-year-old male, was incarcerated for a violent crime committed during a robbery. He had a history of substance abuse, experienced childhood trauma, and had been in and out of the criminal justice system since his teenage years.

Understanding Offending Populations:

1. Substance Abuse and Addiction:
   - Michael's substance abuse issues significantly contributed to his criminal behavior.
   - Understanding the connection between substance abuse and criminality allowed for targeted interventions to address his addiction and related behaviors.
2. Childhood Trauma and Adverse Childhood Experiences (ACEs):
   - Michael had a traumatic childhood, characterized by physical abuse, neglect, and domestic violence.
   - Recognizing the impact of childhood trauma on his behavior provided insights into the need for trauma-informed care and the importance of healing from past experiences.
3. Antisocial Personality Traits:
   - Michael exhibited traits of antisocial personality disorder, including a disregard for the rights of others, impulsivity, and a lack of empathy.
   - Recognizing these traits helped tailor therapeutic approaches to address his specific needs and challenges.

Correctional Psychotherapy Process:

1. Assessment and Treatment Planning:
   - Michael underwent a comprehensive assessment to identify his psychological needs, trauma history, and pattern of violent behavior.
   - The treatment plan focused on addressing trauma, substance abuse, and developing prosocial skills.

2. Trauma-Focused Therapy:
   - Michael engaged in trauma-focused therapy modalities, such as trauma-focused cognitive behavioral therapy (TF-CBT) and eye movement desensitization and reprocessing (EMDR), to process and heal from his traumatic experiences.
   - This therapy aimed to reduce his trauma symptoms, increase emotional regulation, and facilitate behavioral change.

3. Cognitive Behavioral Therapy (CBT):
   - Michael participated in CBT to address his distorted thinking patterns, develop problem-solving skills, and enhance empathetic responses.
   - CBT interventions focused on strategies to manage anger, improve emotional regulation, and foster healthier cognitive processes.

4. Relapse Prevention and Reintegration Planning:
   - Michael received relapse prevention education and support to prevent a return to criminal behavior after release.
   - Reintegration planning involved connecting him with community resources, employment opportunities, and ongoing therapy to support his successful reintegration into society.

Outcomes:

1. Increased Self-Reflection and Accountability:
   - Through correctional psychotherapy, Michael developed a heightened sense of self-reflection, taking accountability for his actions and understanding the consequences of his behavior on others.

2. Effective Coping Strategies and Emotional Regulation:
   - Michael acquired healthier coping mechanisms to manage stressors and triggers, reducing reliance on aggressive or impulsive behavior.
   - He learned emotional regulation skills, enabling him to channel emotions constructively and regulate responses in challenging situations.

3. Reduced Recidivism Risk:
   - The comprehensive correctional psychotherapy tailored to Michael's needs significantly reduced his likelihood of reoffending.
   - Therapy helped address underlying trauma, substance abuse issues, and antisocial behaviors, promoting a healthier and more prosocial lifestyle.

This case study emphasizes the importance of understanding offender populations and implementing tailored correctional psychotherapy interventions. By recognizing the diverse characteristics and underlying factors contributing to criminal behavior, professionals can develop targeted interventions that support individuals like Michael on their rehabilitation journey. Correctional psychotherapy, combining trauma-focused therapy, cognitive behavioral techniques, and reintegration planning play a pivotal role in facilitating positive change, reducing the risk of recidivism, and enabling successful community integration for individuals within the correctional system.

Understanding Offending Populations and the Power of Correctional Psychotherapy—Unlocking Insights is a comprehensive and enlightening book that delves into the intricacies surrounding offending behavior and the transformative potential of correctional psychotherapy. This book provides readers with a deep understanding of the complex factors underlying criminal behavior and highlights the effectiveness of psychotherapeutic interventions in promoting lasting change and offender rehabilitation.

The book begins by exploring the diverse characteristics and risk factors associated with offending populations. It examines the intersection of multiple factors, including socioeconomic background, educational attainment, childhood adversity, and mental health issues, that contributes to the likelihood of engaging in criminal behavior. By unraveling these risk factors, readers gain valuable insights into the nuanced challenges faced by individuals within the criminal justice system.

Drawing on research and case studies, the book highlights the crucial role of correctional psychotherapy in addressing the root causes of criminal behavior. It explores various evidence-based therapeutic approaches, such as cognitive behavioral therapy, psychodynamic therapy, and group therapy, and illuminates their effectiveness in reducing recidivism rates and fostering positive behavioral changes among offenders. Through detailed discussions and practical examples, readers are introduced to the therapeutic techniques and interventions that can facilitate offender rehabilitation and support individuals in their journey toward successful reintegration into society.

Moreover, the book delves into the ethical considerations and challenges inherent in providing psychotherapy within the criminal justice system. It examines issues such as confidentiality, dual relationships, power dynamics, and cultural sensitivity, helping clinicians navigate the complexities of working with this unique population. By addressing these challenges, the book provides valuable guidance and best practices for therapists, ensuring the delivery of ethical and effective correctional psychotherapy.

Furthermore, the book examines the role of collaboration and multidisciplinary approaches in offender rehabilitation. It emphasizes the importance of partnerships among mental health professionals, correctional staff, probation officers, and community services to create a seamless continuum of care throughout the rehabilitation process. By fostering collaboration and coordination, the book advocates for a comprehensive and holistic approach to offender rehabilitation that maximizes positive outcomes.

Overall, *Understanding Offending Populations and the Power of Correctional Psychotherapy—Unlocking Insights* is an indispensable resource for mental health professionals, researchers, policymakers, and anyone interested in helping offenders transform their lives. By unlocking insights into the characteristics of offending populations and the potential of psychotherapeutic interventions, this book inspires a renewed commitment to understanding and addressing the complexities of criminal behavior, ultimately contributing to the advancement of offender rehabilitation and the creation of safer and more just societies.

References

Andrews, D. A., & Bonta, J. (2010). *The psychology of criminal conduct*. Routledge.

Barnao, M., Newman, L. E., Birgden, A., & Porter, T. (2017). Offending diversity and specialty courts: Potential solutions for disproportionate indigenous and female incarcerations. *Psychiatry, Psychology and Law, 24*(1), 130–143.

Corrado, R. R., & Roesch, R. (2017). *Young offenders: Development, intervention, and service needs*. Springer.

Latessa, E. J. (2012). Reviving rehabilitation: The history, policies, and future of correctional reform. *Federal Probation, 76*(2), 47–56.

Palmer, E., McGuire, J., & Kenney, R. (2017). *From supervision to reintegration: Pathways and principles for effective offender reentry*. Routledge.

Chapter 2
Multifaceted Nature of Criminal Behavior

Understanding offending populations and the power of correctional psychotherapy is critical in addressing the complex issues of criminal behavior. Criminal behavior is a complex phenomenon influenced by a variety of factors that interact in intricate ways to shape an individual's propensity to engage in illegal activities. As such, the psychology of criminal conduct provides valuable insights into the motivations and psychological processes that drive individuals to engage in criminal activities (Andrews & Bonta, 2010). By understanding the multifaceted nature of criminal behavior, it becomes possible to develop interventions and treatment strategies that target the specific needs of different offender populations, prevent crime, and promote rehabilitation. This chapter aims to explore the diverse factors that contribute to criminal behavior, including biological, psychological, and sociological influences, illustrating the complexity of this phenomenon.

2.1 Biological Factors and Criminal Behavior

Research has highlighted the potential role of biological factors in predisposing individuals to criminal behavior. Genetic studies have identified specific genes that may contribute to aggressive and antisocial behaviors (Raine, 2013). Additionally, neurological abnormalities, such as impaired impulse control or reduced empathy, have been associated with increased criminal tendencies (Raine, 2013). These biological factors exemplify the intricate interplay between genetics and neurobiology, impacting an individual's susceptibility to engage in criminal conduct.

K. Sapp, *Understanding Offending Populations and the Power of Correctional Psychotherapy*, SpringerBriefs in Offending Populations & Correctional Psychotherapy, https://doi.org/10.1007/978-3-031-45886-6_2

2.1.1 Genetic Influences

Genetic research provides evidence for the influence of genes on criminal behavior. The pioneering work of Raine (2013) suggests that specific genes may contribute to aggressive and antisocial behaviors. Twin studies indicate that genetic factors play a significant role in explaining criminality, with heritability estimates ranging from 40% to 70% (Rutter, 2005). These findings suggest a genetic predisposition to criminal behavior, although it is essential to note that genes alone do not determine criminality but interact with other factors.

2.1.2 Neurological Abnormalities

Neurological abnormalities have been associated with an increased propensity for criminal behavior. Research conducted by Raine (2013) identified impairments in brain regions responsible for impulse control, emotion regulation, and decision-making in individuals with a history of criminal activities. Reduced activity in the prefrontal cortex and abnormal functioning in the amygdala have been observed in individuals engaged in criminal behavior (Raine, 2013). These neurological abnormalities may contribute to poor impulse control, diminished empathy, and an increased likelihood of engaging in criminal acts.

2.1.3 Physiological Factors

Physiological factors, such as hormonal imbalances, have also been linked to criminal behavior. Studies have found an association between testosterone levels and aggression, with higher levels of testosterone being correlated with increased aggressive behavior and a higher likelihood of engaging in criminal activities (Dabbs, 2000). Additionally, low levels of serotonin, a neurotransmitter involved in regulating impulse control and emotional stability, have been implicated in aggressive and impulsive behaviors (Kruesi et al., 1991). These physiological factors can influence an individual's propensity for criminal behavior by altering their emotional and behavioral responses to social stimuli.

2.1.4 Gene–Environment Interactions

It is important to recognize that biological factors interact with environmental influences to shape criminal behavior. Gene–environment interactions play a significant role in modulating the expression of genetic predispositions (Caspi et al., 2002). For example, an individual with a genetic predisposition toward aggression may be more likely to exhibit criminal behavior if exposed to a violent or abusive environment. The interplay between genetic factors and the social environment further highlights the complex nature of criminal behavior.

2.1.5 Conclusion

Biological factors, including genetics, neurological abnormalities, and physiological influences, contribute to the understanding of criminal behavior. Genetic predispositions, neurological impairments, and hormonal imbalances can interact to increase the likelihood of engaging in criminal activities. However, it is crucial to consider the interactions between biological factors and other elements, such as psychological and sociological factors, to develop a comprehensive understanding of criminal behavior. By recognizing the role of biological factors, policymakers, researchers, and practitioners can develop targeted interventions that address the root causes and promote rehabilitation in individuals with a predisposition toward criminal behavior.

2.2 Psychological Factors and Criminal Behavior

Psychological factors play a significant role in the development of criminal behavior. Childhood trauma, for instance, has been linked to an increased likelihood of criminal involvement later in life (Bernet et al., 2012). Poor impulse control, personality disorders, and psychopathy also contribute to the propensity for criminal behavior (Hare, 1999). These psychological factors interact with a person's cognitive, emotional, and motivational processes, shaping their decision-making and behavioral patterns.

2.2.1 Childhood Experiences

Psychological factors, particularly adverse childhood experiences, have a significant impact on the development of criminal behavior. Research suggests that individuals who have experienced neglect, abuse, or trauma during childhood are at a higher risk of engaging in criminal activities later in life (Widom, 1989). These adverse experiences can disrupt healthy psychological development, leading to impaired impulse control, emotional dysregulation, and a limited range of coping strategies, increasing the likelihood of criminal behavior (Afifi et al., 2008).

2.2.2 *Personality Traits*

Certain personality traits have been associated with an increased propensity for criminal behavior. For instance, individuals with antisocial personality disorder exhibit a pattern of disregard for others' rights and a lack of empathy or remorse, making them more prone to engage in criminal activities (American Psychiatric Association, 2013). Other personality traits linked to criminal behavior include impulsivity, sensation-seeking, and low agreeableness (Miller & Lynam, 2003). These traits influence an individual's decision-making processes, self-control, and inclination toward risk-taking, contributing to their involvement in criminal acts.

2.2.3 *Cognitive Processes*

Cognitive processes, such as cognitive distortions and rationalizations, also play a role in criminal behavior. Individuals engaging in criminal activities often exhibit faulty thinking patterns that justify their actions, minimize the consequences, or blame others (Ellis & Walsh, 2007). Cognitive distortions, including beliefs in entitlement, hostility, or the need for excitement, can further reinforce a criminal mindset (Walters & White, 2010). These cognitive processes influence an individual's interpretation of events, their moral reasoning, and their inclination to engage in illegal behaviors.

2.2.4 *Interaction of Psychological Factors*

It is important to recognize that psychological factors interact with one another to contribute to criminal behavior. Adverse childhood experiences can affect the development of personality traits, shaping an individual's emotional and behavioral responses to environmental stimuli (Afifi et al., 2008). Personality traits, in turn, influence how individuals interpret and process information, influencing their cog nitive processes and decision-making (Miller & Lynam, 2003). The interaction between these psychological factors creates a complex dynamic that underlies criminal behavior.

2.2.5 *Conclusion*

Psychological factors play a significant role in the development of criminal behavior. Adverse childhood experiences, personality traits, and cognitive processes contribute to an individual's susceptibility to engage in illegal activities. By understanding these psychological factors, policymakers, researchers, and practitioners can design targeted interventions that address the root causes and promote rehabilitation. Effective interventions can include trauma-informed therapies, cognitive behavioral interventions, and programs aimed at fostering prosocial behaviors, ultimately reducing the likelihood of criminal recidivism.

2.3 Sociological Factors and Criminal Behavior

Sociological factors, such as socioeconomic disadvantage, social disorganization, and peer influences, also contribute to criminal behavior. Individuals from impoverished backgrounds may turn to criminal activities as a means of survival or achieving material gains (Sampson & Laub, 1993). Furthermore, weak social bonds, lack of positive role models, and exposure to deviant peer groups increase the likelihood of engaging in criminal behavior (Akers et al., 1979). Societal factors furnish the context within which criminal behavior pervades, demonstrating the interplay between individual behavior and the broader social environment.

2.3.1 Socioeconomic Status

Socioeconomic status plays a crucial role in shaping criminal behavior. Individuals from disadvantaged backgrounds, characterized by poverty, limited access to resources, and educational opportunities, face higher risks of engaging in criminal activities (Sampson & Laub, 1993). Economic strain, coupled with a lack of legitimate opportunities for socioeconomic mobility, can incentivize individuals to turn to illicit activities as a means for survival or economic gain (Messner & Rosenfeld, 2017). The socioeconomic context within which individuals live significantly impacts their likelihood of involvement in criminal behavior.

2.3.2 Neighborhood Disadvantage

Neighborhood characteristics and social disorganization are important sociological factors in understanding criminal behavior. Empirical research suggests that residing in neighborhoods marked by high rates of poverty, unemployment, residential instability, and social disorder increases the risk of criminal engagement (Sampson, 2012). Weak social ties, inadequate social control mechanisms, and limited availability of resources within disadvantaged neighborhoods contribute to higher levels of criminal behavior (Sampson & Laub, 1993).

2.3.3 Peer Influence

Peers and social networks have a powerful impact on the development of criminal behavior. The association with deviant peers who engage in criminal activities increases an individual's likelihood of engaging in similar behaviors (Akers et al., 1979). Peer influences can involve direct involvement in criminal acts, modeling of delinquent behaviors, or social pressure to conform to deviant norms (Thornberry & Krohn, 2003). The influence of peers on criminal behavior underscores the significance of social interactions and the need to consider the social environment in understanding criminal conduct.

2.3.4 Interaction of Sociological Factors

Sociological factors do not operate in isolation; they interact and reinforce one another. For instance, socioeconomic disadvantage and neighborhood characteristics can lead to the formation of deviant peer networks, further perpetuating criminal behavior (Sampson & Laub, 1993). The interplay between these sociological factors creates a cycle whereby individuals are exposed to disadvantageous environments, adopt deviant behaviors through peer influences, and subsequently shape their own social environments, perpetuating the cycle of criminal behavior.

2.3.5 Conclusion

Sociological factors significantly influence the development of criminal behavior. Socioeconomic status, neighborhood disadvantage, and peer influences all contribute to an individual's likelihood of engaging in illegal activities. Understanding these sociological factors is essential for developing effective interventions that address the root causes of criminal behavior. Policies that aim to reduce socioeconomic disparities improve community resources and provide positive social support systems that play a vital role in preventing criminal behavior and promoting a safer society.

2.4 Interaction of Multiple Factors

It is crucial to recognize that criminal behavior does not stem from a single determinant but arises from the complex interaction of various factors. Biological predispositions can interact with adverse childhood experiences to increase the risk of criminal behaviors (Bernet et al., 2012). Furthermore, sociological factors can exacerbate the influence of psychological factors, leading individuals with poor impulse control to connect with deviant peer groups, ultimately amplifying their engagement in criminal activities (Akers et al., 1979). It is the intricate interplay between these various factors that contributes to the multifaceted nature of criminal behavior.

2.4.1 Interplay of Multiple Factors

Behavior is influenced by various factors, including biological, psychological, and sociological dimensions. These factors do not act in isolation; rather, they interact with one another to shape behavior. For instance, genetic predispositions may interact with environmental factors, such as parenting style or access to resources, to influence personality traits and behavioral tendencies (Caspi et al., 2003). Similarly, psychological factors, such as cognitive processes and emotional states, can interact with sociological factors, such as peer influences or cultural norms, to influence behavior (Bronfenbrenner, 1979). Understanding these complex interactions is crucial for comprehending the multifaceted nature of behavior.

2.4.2 Cumulative Effects of Multiple Factors

The effects of multiple factors are often cumulative, meaning that their influence accumulates over time and interacts to shape behavior. Each individual factor contributes to a person's development and may have different strengths or effects at various stages of life. For example, adverse childhood experiences, combined with genetic vulnerabilities, can lead to continued behavioral problems into adolescence and adulthood (Caspi et al., 2002). As individuals navigate through different environments and experiences, the cumulative effects of these factors intensify and manifest in behavior. By considering the cumulative effect, we gain a more comprehensive understanding of behavior and its underlying determinants.

2.4.3 Interactions Between Factors

The interplay between multiple factors involves complex interactions and feedback loops. Biological factors may influence psychological processes, such as brain functioning or neurotransmitter imbalances, which in turn affect behavior (Moffitt et al., 2005). Psychological factors, such as self-perception or cognitive biases, can influence the interpretation and response to sociological factors, such as peer pressure or societal norms (Bandura, 1986). The interaction between these factors can further reinforce or mitigate their effects, resulting in a dynamic and evolving process that shapes behavior over time.

2.4.4 Developmental Trajectories

The interplay and cumulative effects of multiple factors are particularly evident in developmental trajectories. As individuals progress through life, their exposure to different influences and experiences can lead to significant changes in behavior. Early childhood experiences, such as parenting styles or socioeconomic status, can set the foundation for subsequent developmental outcomes (Bronfenbrenner, 1979). These early influences interact with ongoing factors, such as education, relationships, and societal factors, shaping behavior throughout the life span. Understanding the cumulative effects of these factors across different developmental stages is essential for predicting and intervening in behavioral trajectories.

2.4.5 Conclusion

Human behavior is influenced by a complex interplay of multiple factors, including biological, psychological, and sociological dimensions. These factors do not act in isolation but rather interact and accumulate in their effects on behavior. By comprehensively examining the interplay and cumulative effects of these factors, we can better understand the complexity and variability of human behavior. This knowledge is vital for developing interventions and policies that address the underlying determinants of behavior and promote positive outcomes for individuals and society as a whole.

2.5 Conclusion

Criminal behavior emerges from the interplay of multiple factors, including biological, psychological, and sociological influences. Genetic predispositions, neurological abnormalities, adverse childhood experiences, personality traits, socioeconomic status, neighborhood disadvantage, and peer influences all contribute to an individual's likelihood of engaging in criminal acts. By acknowledging and incorporating these multifactorial influences, policymakers, researchers, and practitioners can adopt a holistic approach to preventing and addressing criminal behavior effectively. Interventions targeting biological, psychological, and sociological factors can provide a more comprehensive solution to reducing crime rates and promoting rehabilitation within society.

References

Afifi, T. O., Enns, M. W., Cox, B. J., Asmundson, G. J., Stein, M. B., & Sareen, J. (2008). Population attributable fractions of psychiatric disorders and suicide ideation and attempts associated with adverse childhood experiences. *American Journal of Public Health, 98*(5), 946–952.

Akers, R. L., Krohn, M. D., Lanza-Kaduce, L., & Radosevich, M. (1979). Social learning and deviant behavior: A specific test of a general theory. *American Sociological Review, 44*(4), 636–655.

American Psychiatric Association. (2013). *Diagnostic and statistical manual of mental disorders* (5th ed.). American Psychiatric Publishing.

Andrews, D. A., & Bonta, J. (2010). *The psychology of criminal conduct* (5th ed.). Routledge.

Bandura, A. (1986). *Social foundations of thought and action: A social cognitive theory.* Prentice Hall.

Bernet, W., Vnencak-Jones, C. L., & Farooq, U. (2012). Antisocial personality disorder and criminal justice: An introduction. *Journal of the American Academy of Psychiatry and the Law, 40*(3), 285–288.

Bronfenbrenner, U. (1979). *The ecology of human development: Experiments by nature and design*. Harvard University Press.

Caspi, A., McClay, J., Moffitt, T. E., Mill, J., Martin, J., Craig, I. W., Taylor, A., & Poulton, R. (2002). Role of genotype in the cycle of violence in maltreated children. *Science, 297*(5582), 851–854.

Caspi, A., Sugden, K., Moffitt, T. E., Taylor, A., Craig, I. W., Harrington, H., McClay, J., Mill, J., Martin, J., Braithwaite, A., & Poulton, R. (2003). Influence of life stress on depression: Moderation by a polymorphism in the 5-HTT gene. *Science, 301*(5631), 386–389.

Dabbs, J. M., Jr. (2000). *Heroes, rogues, and lovers: Testosterone and behavior*. McGraw-Hill.

Ellis, T. E., & Walsh, A. (2007). *Criminology: A global perspective*. Allyn & Bacon.

Hare, R. D. (1999). *Without conscience: The disturbing world of the psychopaths among us.* Guilford Press.

Kruesi, M. J. P., Rapoport, J. L., Hamburger, S., Hibbs, E., & Potter, W. Z. (1991). Cerebrospinal fluid monoamine metabolites, aggression, and impulsivity in disruptive behavior disorders of children and adolescents. *Archives of General Psychiatry, 48*(9), 901–907.

Messner, S. F., & Rosenfeld, R. (2017). *Crime and the American dream.* Cengage Learning.

Miller, J. D., & Lynam, D. R. (2003). Psychopathy and the five-factor model of personality: A replication and extension. *Journal of Personality Assessment, 81*(2), 168–178.

Moffitt, T. E., Caspi, A., & Rutter, M. (2005). Strategy for investigating interactions between measured genes and measured environments. *Archives of General Psychiatry, 62*(5), 473–481.

Raine, A. (2013). *The anatomy of violence: The biological roots of crime*. Vintage.

Rutter, M. (2005). Environmentally mediated risks for psychopathology: Research strategies and findings. *Journal of the American Academy of Child & Adolescent Psychiatry, 44*(1), 3–18.

Sampson, R. J. (2012). *Great American city: Chicago and the enduring neighborhood effect.* University of Chicago Press.

Sampson, R. J., & Laub, J. H. (1993). *Crime in the making: Pathways and turning points through life*. Harvard University Press.

Thornberry, T. P., & Krohn, M. D. (2003). *Taking stock of delinquency: An overview of findings from contemporary longitudinal studies*. Springer.

Walters, G. D., & White, T. F. (2010). *The criminal lifestyle: Patterns of serious criminal conduct.* SAGE Publications.

Widom, C. S. (1989). The cycle of violence. *Science, 244*(4901), 160–166.

Chapter 3
Exploring the Offending Puzzle: Unveiling the Characteristics of the Offending Populations

Correctional psychotherapy is an essential component of the criminal justice system, aiming to address the underlying causes of criminal behavior and facilitate rehabilitation (Andrews & Bonta, 2010a, b). The offending population within correctional facilities consists of individuals who have committed various offenses, from nonviolent crimes to serious felony charges (Bureau of Justice Statistics, 2020). These individuals often deal with complex psychosocial issues such as substance abuse, mental health, and personality disorders (Andrews & Bonta, 2010a, b). Correctional psychotherapy targets these underlying issues through evidence-based interventions and provides the offenders with the necessary skills and support for successful reintegration into society (Martin, 2001). By working with this population, correctional psychotherapists are crucial in reducing recidivism rates and promoting a safer community (Andrews & Bonta, 2010a, b).

3.1 Offending Populations Defined

Offending populations are diverse and have different backgrounds, circumstances, and experiences. It is essential to recognize that numerous factors contribute to criminal behavior, and understanding these factors is crucial to developing effective interventions that can prevent future offender behavior. Research has identified some potential risk factors or characteristics associated with criminal behavior. However, these factors are not deterministic and do not apply to everyone who engages in offending behavior. These factors include:

- Childhood experiences: Individuals who have experienced abuse or neglect in childhood or have grown up in households with high levels of conflict or substance abuse may be at increased risk for engaging in criminal behavior later in life.

K. Sapp, *Understanding Offending Populations and the Power of Correctional Psychotherapy*, SpringerBriefs in Offending Populations & Correctional Psychotherapy, https://doi.org/10.1007/978-3-031-45886-6_3

- Mental health issues: Mental health conditions, such as mood disorders, anxiety disorders, or personality disorders, may contribute to criminal behavior.
- Substance abuse: Substance abuse, particularly drugs or alcohol, has been identified as a risk factor for criminal behavior.
- Lack of social support: Individuals who lack social support, whether due to social isolation or poor relationships with family or peers, may be at increased risk of engaging in criminal behavior.
- Poverty and socioeconomic disadvantage: A lack of access to education, healthcare, and employment opportunities, as well as living in areas with high levels of crime and violence, have been identified as risk factors for criminal behavior.

Understanding the characteristics and needs of different offending populations is crucial for effective corrective interventions. This section aims to provide a comprehensive definition of various offending populations found within the criminal justice system. By examining these populations' demographic, contextual, and behavioral factors, we can gain insight into the complexities of offending populations.

3.1.1 Juvenile Offenders

Juvenile offenders, also known as delinquent youth, constitute a distinct subgroup within the offending population. They are individuals who have engaged in delinquent behavior under 18, as defined by the legal system in many jurisdictions. These young offenders may display a range of offenses, including theft, substance abuse, violence, and gang involvement (Abram et al., 2014). Studies have shown that many juvenile offenders exhibit mental health problems such as conduct disorders, substance abuse, and mood disorders (Abram et al., 2014). Understanding juvenile offenders' unique characteristics and needs is critical for developing effective interventions and rehabilitation efforts.

Juvenile offenders are at a unique stage of development, with distinct cognitive, emotional, and social needs. Many studies suggest that impulsivity, poor self-control, susceptibility to peer influence, and limited problem-solving skills contribute to delinquent behavior among juveniles (Moffitt, 1993). Understanding the specific challenges this developmental stage poses is essential for tailoring interventions accordingly.

Juvenile offenders often face various risk factors contributing to their involvement in delinquency. These risk factors include adverse childhood experiences (e.g., abuse, neglect), family dysfunction, academic difficulties, substance abuse, and association with delinquent peers (Ferdon et al., 2013). Exploring and addressing these underlying risk factors is crucial for designing effective prevention and intervention strategies.

Given juvenile offenders' distinct characteristics and developmental needs, an emphasis on rehabilitation is a central component of juvenile justice systems in many countries. The focus is often on addressing the underlying causes of delinquent behavior, providing therapeutic interventions, and promoting successful reintegration into society. Programs commonly employ cognitive behavioral interventions, individual and family counseling, education, and skill-building activities to address the specific needs of juvenile offenders (Welsh et al., 2017).

Legal frameworks governing the treatment of juvenile offenders often differ from those applied to adult offenders. Juvenile justice systems typically adopt a less punitive and more rehabilitative approach. Juvenile offenders may be subject to diversion programs, community-based interventions, or, in some cases, secure residential facilities for education, treatment, and reform. Balancing accountability, rehabilitation, and public safety is vital in the juvenile justice system.

Efforts to prevent juvenile delinquency and intervene early are crucial in addressing the needs of at-risk youth. Diverting potential offenders from the formal juvenile justice system through community-based diversion programs and early intervention initiatives and promoting positive youth development can help reduce the likelihood of subsequent offenses (Pardini et al., 2014). Recognizing and addressing risk factors during childhood and early adolescence are pivotal in preventing future delinquent behavior.

Ultimately, juvenile offenders form a distinct subgroup within the offending population and are characterized by their developmental stage, unique risk factors, and specialized interventions. Understanding juvenile offenders' specific challenges allows for developing practical rehabilitative approaches that address underlying causes and promote successful community reintegration. By focusing on prevention, early intervention, and evidence-based practices, society can reduce delinquency rates, support at-risk youth, and foster positive youth development.

3.1.2 Adult Offenders

Adult offenders constitute a diverse subgroup within the offending population, encompassing individuals who have reached the age of majority and engaged in criminal behavior. Understanding the characteristics, risk factors, and treatment needs specific to adult offenders is crucial for tailoring interventions and promoting successful rehabilitation efforts.

Encompassing various backgrounds, age groups, genders, ethnicities, and offense types, adult offenders may be involved in property crimes, drug offenses, violent offenses, or a combination of these. The diversity within this population necessitates a comprehensive understanding of the factors contributing to adult criminal behavior (Fazel et al., 2006).

Many adult offenders exhibit various risk factors contributing to their involvement in criminal behavior. These factors include a history of substance abuse, mental health problems, childhood trauma, socioeconomic disadvantage, and limited educational or employment opportunities (Brennan et al., 2012). Identifying and addressing these risk factors are essential for effective treatment and rehabilitation.

Successful reentry into the community is an important goal for adult offenders. This process involves providing support and resources to facilitate their reintegration into society, addressing practical needs (such as housing and employment), and promoting prosocial connections. Comprehensive reentry programs incorporating case management, vocational training, and community-based support have shown promising results in reducing recidivism among this population.

Adult offenders represent a diverse subgroup within the offending population, requiring tailored interventions that address their characteristics and criminogenic needs. Understanding the diversity of offenses, risk factors, and treatment considerations is vital for designing effective interventions to reduce recidivism rates and promote successful reintegration into society. Using evidence-based approaches and comprehensive reentry programs contributes to the rehabilitation and successful community reintegration of adult offenders.

3.1.3 Special Offending Populations

Specific offender subgroups require specialized attention due to their unique characteristics and needs. These include female offenders, LGBTQIA2S offenders, sex offenders, individuals with intellectual or developmental disabilities, and those with serious mental illnesses (SMIs).

3.1.3.1 Female Offenders

Female offenders represent a unique subgroup within the criminal justice system. Understanding female offenders' unique characteristics, risk factors, and needs is crucial for developing effective and gender-responsive interventions that address their specific circumstances. Female offenders often have a higher prevalence of trauma and victimization experiences than male offenders. Many have a history of physical, sexual, or emotional abuse, usually starting in childhood (Bloom et al., 2003). The effects of trauma can contribute to their involvement in criminal behavior, highlighting the importance of trauma-informed care and interventions.

Many female offenders have co-occurring substance abuse and mental health disorders. Substance abuse can be a coping mechanism for trauma and contribute to criminal behavior (Sacks et al., 2014). Addressing substance abuse and providing comprehensive mental health services are vital to effective interventions for female offenders. Many female offenders are mothers, and their involvement in the criminal justice system can harm their children. Maintaining connections with their children and addressing parenting needs are crucial for promoting positive outcomes and reducing intergenerational involvement in the criminal justice system (Eddy & Poehlmann, 2010).

Female offenders benefit from gender-responsive interventions that consider their unique needs, strengths, and challenges. Gender-responsive approaches recognize the impact of gender socialization, trauma, and victimization on female offenders' lives. They emphasize empowerment, building healthy relationships, addressing trauma, and tackling gender-specific issues (Bloom et al., 2003). Successful reentry into the community is critical for female offenders. Women-specific reentry programs that address housing, employment, education, healthcare, and reunification can support their transition and reduce recidivism (Eddy & Poehlmann, 2010). Collaborating with community organizations to provide comprehensive support is critical to their thriving community integration.

Female offenders form a unique subgroup within the criminal justice system, requiring gender-responsive interventions that address their unique experiences and needs. Trauma-informed care, addressing co-occurring substance abuse and mental health issues, supporting maternal roles, and providing tailored reentry programs are essential to effective interventions for female offenders. By adopting gender-responsive practices, society can promote the rehabilitation and successful reintegration of female offenders into their communities.

3.1.3.2 LGBTQIA2S+ Offenders

The LGBTQIA2S+ community, consisting of individuals identifying as lesbian, gay, bisexual, transgender, queer, intersex, asexual, or two-spirit plus more, can face unique challenges within the criminal justice system. Recognizing the specific needs and experiences of LGBTQIA2S+ offenders is essential for developing inclusive and effective interventions that address their circumstances.

LGBTQIA2S+ individuals can be targets of discrimination, harassment, and violence, which may contribute to their involvement in the criminal justice system. Experiences of homophobia, transphobia, and gender-based violence can impact mental health and increase the risk of criminal behavior (Lynch & Meyer, 2012). It is crucial to consider these contextual factors when working with LGBTQIA2S+ offenders.

Research suggests that LGBTQIA2S individuals may be overrepresented in the criminal justice system, often due to heightened exposure to risk factors such as homelessness, substance abuse, and mental health issues (Mallon, 2019). Disparities exist in sentencing, treatment, and access to supportive services, necessitating a nuanced approach to address the specific needs of LGBTQIA2S+ offenders.

LGBTQIA2S+ offenders may have intersecting identities, such as race, ethnicity, and socioeconomic status, which can further compound their experiences within the criminal justice system. Intersectionality recognizes the overlapping nature of social identities and emphasizes the need for comprehensive, culturally sensitive interventions that address the complexities of these individuals' lives (Crenshaw, 1989).

Creating safe and inclusive environments within correctional settings is crucial for LGBTQIA2S+ offenders. This involves adopting policies that protect against discrimination, harassment, and violence based on gender identity or sexual orientation. Training correctional staff and providing resources that promote cultural competence and understanding of LGBTQIA2S+ issues can significantly enhance the effectiveness of interventions (Mallon, 2019).

Many LGBTQIA2S+ individuals have experienced significant trauma related to their sexual or gender identity, including family rejection, bullying, or hate crimes. Trauma-informed approaches emphasize understanding these experiences and providing supportive, trauma-sensitive interventions that avoid retraumatization (Ford & Blaustein, 2013). Incorporating trauma-informed care is vital when working with LGBTQIA2S offenders within the criminal justice system.

As such, LGBTQIA2S+ offenders represent a particular offending population, facing unique challenges within the criminal justice system. Understanding the contexts of discrimination, victimization, disparities, and intersecting identities is essential for providing effective interventions that address their specific needs and promote successful rehabilitation. Creating safe and inclusive environments, adopting trauma-informed care, and valuing intersectionality are crucial steps in supporting the successful outcomes of LGBTQIA2S+ individuals in the criminal justice system.

3.1.3.3 Sex Offenders

Sex offenders represent a unique and specialized subgroup within the offending population. They have been convicted of offenses related to sexual misconduct, which may include various forms of sexual assault, child pornography, or other sexually exploitative behaviors. Understanding the characteristics, risk factors, and treatment needs specific to this population is crucial for developing effective interventions and enhancing community safety.

Sex offenders can be classified into different categories based on factors such as the age of the victim, the relationship with the victim, and the nature of the offense. These categories may include pedophilic offenders (who victimize children), incest offenders (who victimize family members), or nonfamilial adult offenders (who victimize adults). Each group has risk factors and treatment considerations (Hanson et al., 2020).

Risk assessment is crucial for the effective management and treatment of sex offenders. Assessment tools, such as the Static-99R and the Sex Offender Risk Appraisal Guide (SORAG), help determine an individual's likelihood of reoffending and inform risk management strategies (Hanson & Thornton, 2000). Differential treatment approaches, based on risk levels, can target specific needs and mitigate the risk of reoffending. Treatment for sex offenders typically relies on specialized interventions to reduce risk and facilitate rehabilitation. Cognitive behavioral therapy (CBT) and relapse prevention approaches are commonly utilized to address distorted thinking patterns, develop empathy, and enhance self-regulation skills (Ward & Beech, 2006). Additional treatment components may include trauma-informed therapy, social skills training, and psychoeducational programs focused on developing healthy attitudes and behaviors.

Successful community reintegration is a primary goal in the management of sex offenders. This process requires a collaborative approach involving correctional professionals, mental health providers, and community support services. Supervision programs, such as sex offender registration and notification, coupled with ongoing treatment and monitoring, support the gradual reintegration of individuals into society while maintaining community safety. Treating sex offenders requires striking a balance between promoting rehabilitation and mitigating the potential risk to the community. This challenge necessitates ongoing evaluation and monitoring to ensure effective treatment interventions and public safety remains a priority. The development and implementation of evidence-based practices and the collaboration between correctional and mental health professionals are essential in managing this delicate balance.

Sex offenders represent a specialized subgroup within the offending population due to the nature of their offenses and associated risks. Understanding the specific characteristics, risk assessment, treatment considerations, and community reintegration of sex offenders is essential for implementing effective interventions and maintaining public safety. By adopting evidence-based practices and employing a multidisciplinary approach, society can work toward reducing recidivism rates, promoting offender rehabilitation, and ensuring the well-being of potential victims.

3.1.3.4 Offenders with Intellectual or Developmental Disabilities

Offenders with intellectual or developmental disabilities represent a vulnerable subgroup within the criminal justice system. Intellectual or developmental disabilities (IDD) are conditions that begin in childhood and affects an individual's cognitive abilities, social skills, and daily functioning, which can be attributed to various factors, including genetic conditions, prenatal exposure to toxins or infections, birth complications, and certain medical conditions. Additionally, environmental factors and social influences can also impact the development and manifestation of intellectual or developmental disabilities. These individuals often face challenges in understanding the legal system, communicating effectively, and comprehending the consequences of their actions. Tailored interventions that address their cognitive abilities provide appropriate accommodations and consider their specific needs are necessary for effective rehabilitation.

Individuals with IDD have limitations in cognitive functioning, which may impact their understanding of the legal system, decision-making abilities, and comprehension of the consequences of their actions. Individuals with IDD typically have below-average intellectual abilities, as measured by standardized test of intelligence quotient (IQ). The severity of symptoms can vary among individuals and may range from mild to severe. Adaptive functioning, including social and practical skills, can also be affected, making it difficult for them to navigate and meet the demands of correctional settings (Lindsay et al., 2014).

Many individuals with IDD experience challenges in communication, including expressive and receptive language abilities. This can affect their ability to participate in legal proceedings effectively, communicate with correctional staff, and advocate for their needs. Adjustments in communication strategies and access to support services are essential for ensuring fair and effective interactions within the criminal justice system. Individuals with IDD may face increased vulnerability to victimization, exploitation, and abuse due to their cognitive limitations, trusting natures, and potential difficulties in recognizing and reporting victimization. Addressing these risk factors and providing tailored support are crucial to protect this population from further harm (Bigby & Douglas, 2018).

Supportive interventions for offenders with IDD should focus on providing accommodations, adapting communication methods, and addressing specific therapeutic needs. Strategies may include simplified language, visual aids, adaptive technology, and specialized counseling or skills training that cater to their cognitive abilities and learning styles (Lindsay et al., 2014). Collaboration between correctional staff, disability professionals, and community support services is crucial for effective implementation. Considering the unique circumstances of offenders with IDD, diversion programs that aim to redirect individuals away from the criminal justice system and toward appropriate support and services are vital. Collaboration between justice agencies, disability service providers, and community organizations is necessary to develop specialized diversion programs and establish comprehensive support networks to address the specific needs of this population.

Offenders with intellectual or developmental disabilities require specialized interventions and support within the criminal justice system. It is crucial to recognize their unique challenges, provide tailored accommodations, promote effective communication, and address their therapeutic and adaptive needs. By implementing supportive and inclusive practices, society can ensure fair treatment, protect against victimization, and facilitate the successful rehabilitation and reintegration of individuals with IDD into their communities.

3.1.3.5 Offenders with Serious Mental Illness

Offenders with serious mental illness (SMI) constitute a unique subgroup within the criminal justice system. Understanding the specific challenges, needs, and appropriate interventions for this population is crucial for providing effective treatment, reducing recidivism, and facilitating successful reintegration into the community. The prevalence of severe mental illness is higher among individuals involved in the criminal justice system than among the general population. Conditions such as schizophrenia, bipolar disorder, major depressive disorder, and other severe psychiatric disorders are common among this population (Fazel et al., 2006). Risk factors such as limited access to mental health services and co-occurring substance abuse can further complicate their needs.

Offenders with SMI require specialized treatment interventions that address their mental health conditions within the context of their criminal behavior. These interventions should aim to stabilize psychiatric symptoms, reduce the risk of reoffending, and support their recovery and overall functioning (Lamb & Weinberger, 2008). Challenges in providing appropriate treatment include:

- Limited access to mental health resources
- Coordination between correctional and mental health systems
- Ensuring continuity of care during reentry into the community

Successful treatment for offenders with SMI often requires collaboration among mental health professionals, correctional staff, and community-based service providers. A multidisciplinary approach involving psychiatric assessment, medication management, counseling, and therapeutic interventions is necessary to address the complex needs of this population (Skeem et al., 2011). Coordinated case management and interagency collaboration throughout the criminal justice process are vital for providing comprehensive care.

Crisis intervention services, including specialized training for law enforcement and emergency responders, can help divert individuals with SMI from the criminal justice system during mental health crises. Diversion programs, such as mental health courts and specialized treatment programs, aim to provide alternative approaches that address the root causes of criminal behavior while promoting mental health treatment and support (Steadman et al., 2015). Successful reentry into the community for offenders with SMI requires a range of supportive services. This may include transitional housing, mental health treatment, access to healthcare, vocational training, and assistance in obtaining stable employment and social support networks.

Collaboration between correctional systems, mental health agencies, and community stakeholders can facilitate the provision of these comprehensive support systems.

Offenders with serious mental illness have complex needs that require a tailored approach within the criminal justice system. Understanding the prevalence of mental illness, addressing treatment challenges, and promoting collaborative care are crucial for effective intervention and successful reintegration. By implementing crisis intervention programs, diversion initiatives, and comprehensive community support, society can improve outcomes, reduce recidivism, and provide individuals with SMI the opportunity for recovery and stability.

3.2 Conclusion

Understanding and addressing the needs of different offending populations are crucial for effective correctional psychotherapy. This chapter provides a comprehensive definition of various offending populations found within the criminal justice system. Juvenile offenders are characterized by their age and unique developmental issues. Adult offenders represent a diverse group with varying risk factors and criminogenic needs. Special populations, such as female offenders, LGBTQIA2S offenders, sex offenders, individuals with intellectual or developmental disabilities, and those with serious mental illness, require tailored interventions that address their specific characteristics and challenges. Understanding the complexities of these offending populations is fundamental to implementing effective correctional interventions and promoting successful rehabilitation.

References

Abram, K. M., Choe, J. Y., & Washburn, J. J. (2014). Suicidal ideation and behaviors among youths in juvenile detention. *Journal of the American Academy of Child & Adolescent Psychiatry, 53*(6), 684–694.

Andrews, D. A., & Bonta, J. (2010a). *The psychology of criminal conduct* (5th ed.). Routledge.

Andrews, D. A., & Bonta, J. (2010b). Rehabilitating criminal justice policy and practice. *Psychology, Public Policy, and Law, 16*(1), 39–55.

Bigby, C., & Douglas, J. (2018). Offenders with intellectual disability. In S. Taylor & R. Ibbotson (Eds.), *The Lancashire handbook of crime, justice and community safety* (pp. 335–351). Palgrave Macmillan.

Bloom, B., Owen, B., & Covington, S. (2003). *Gender-responsive strategies: Research, practice, and guiding principles for women offenders*. National Institute of Corrections.

Brennan, I. R., Moore, S. C., & Shepherd, J. P. (2012). Risk factors for violent victimization and injury from six years of the British Crime Survey. *International Journal of Injury Control and Safety Promotion, 19*(1), 5–15.

Bureau of Justice Statistics. (2020). *Corrections statistics*. Retrieved from https://www.bjs.gov/index.cfm?ty=tp&tid=17

Crenshaw, K. W. (1989). Demarginalizing the intersection of race and sex: A Black feminist critique of antidiscrimination doctrine, feminist theory and antiracist politics. *University of Chicago Legal Forum, 139*(1), 139–167.

Eddy, J. M., & Poehlmann, J. (2010). *Children of incarcerated parents: A handbook for researchers and practitioners*. Urban Institute Press.

Fazel, S., Bains, P., & Doll, H. (2006). Substance abuse and dependence in prisoners: A systematic review. *Addiction, 101*(2), 181–191.

Ferdon, C., Hertz, M. F., & Huizinga, D. (2013). Protective factors for youth violence perpetration: Findings from the National Longitudinal Study of Adolescent Health. *Journal of Adolescent Health, 52*(1), 21–27.

Ford, J. D., & Blaustein, M. E. (2013). Systemic self-regulation: A framework for trauma-informed services in residential juvenile justice programs. *Journal of Family Violence, 28*(7), 665–677.

Hanson, R. K., & Thornton, D. (2000). Improving risk assessments for sex offenders: A comparison of three actuarial scales. *Law and Human Behavior, 24*(1), 119–136.

Hanson, R. K., Harris, A. J. R., Helmus, L., & Thornton, D. (2020). High–risk sex offenders: Evidence–based adjustment of treatment. *Journal of Interpersonal Violence, 35*(3–4), 813–833.

Lamb, H. R., & Weinberger, L. E. (2008). Persons with severe mental illness in jails and prisons: A review. *Psychiatric Services, 59*(4), 483–492.

Lindsay, W., Carson, D., & O'Brien, G. (2014). Offenders with intellectual and developmental disabilities: Recent research and future directions. *Journal of Applied Research in Intellectual Disabilities, 27*(4), 323–335.

Lynch, S. M., & Meyer, I. H. (2012). Inclusion counts: The economic security of LGBTQ people in the United States. *LGBTQ Policy Journal at the Harvard Kennedy School, 2*(1), 1–25.

Mallon, G. P. (2019). The overrepresentation and experiences of LGBTQ youth in the juvenile justice system. In L. A. Craig, C. Dixon, & J. M. Gault-Sherman (Eds.), *Emerging issues in juvenile justice: Volume 7: LGBTQ youth in the juvenile justice system: Disproportionality and promising interventions* (pp. 61–73). U.S. Department of Justice, Office of Juvenile Justice and Delinquency Prevention.

Martin, D. J. (2001). The effectiveness of group psychotherapy for adult male psychiatric patients convicted of sexual offenses. *International Journal of Offender Therapy and Comparative Criminology, 45*(3), 405–417.

Moffitt, T. E. (1993). Adolescence-limited and life-course-persistent antisocial behavior: A developmental taxonomy. *Psychological Review, 100*(4), 674–701.

Pardini, D. A., Loeber, R., & Stouthamer-Loeber, M. (2014). Developmental shifts in parent and peer influences on boys' beliefs about delinquent behavior. *Journal of Research on Adolescence, 24*(3), 566–580.

Sacks, J. Y., McKendrick, K., & Hamilton, Z. K. (2014). A review of the literature on gender and substance abuse: A focus on treatment outcomes. *Gender Medicine, 11*(6), 445–460.

Skeem, J. L., Manchak, S., & Peterson, J. K. (2011). Correctional policy for offenders with mental illness: Creating a new paradigm for recidivism reduction. *Law and Human Behavior, 35*(2), 110–126.

Steadman, H. J., Morris, S. M., & Dennis, D. L. (2015). The sequential intercept model and criminal justice: Promoting community alternatives for individuals with serious mental illness. *Psychology, Public Policy, and Law, 21*(4), 379–391.

Ward, T., & Beech, A. R. (2006). An integrated theory of sexual offending. *Aggression and Violent Behavior, 11*(1), 44–63.

Welsh, B. C., Sullivan, C. J., & Wurzburg, G. (2017). *Juvenile delinquency: Theory, practice, and law*. Cengage Learning.

Chapter 4
Historical Overview of Correctional Psychotherapy

Correctional psychotherapy, as a specialized form of therapy provided within correctional settings, has its roots in various historical and theoretical foundations and has evolved. Understanding the early origins and influences is crucial for tracing the evolution and development of correctional psychotherapy as a distinct field of practice. This section provides a historical overview of the development and progression of correctional psychotherapy.

4.1 Moral Treatment Movement

The Moral Treatment Movement was a significant historical development that influenced the evolution of mental health care and correctional psychotherapy. It arose during the late eighteenth and early nineteenth centuries as a response to the deplorable conditions and harsh treatment in asylums and prisons. The movement aimed to revolutionize the care and treatment of individuals with mental illness by emphasizing humane, moral practices over punitive approaches. Its proponents, including Philippe Pinel in France and William Tuke in England, advocated for compassionate, respectful care that focused on therapeutic interventions rather than mere confinement or punishment.

The principles of the Moral Treatment Movement sought to create environments that provided dignity, compassionate care, and opportunities for rehabilitation. Individuals with mental illness were seen as deserving of respect and understanding, and their symptoms were viewed as manifestations of a diseased mind rather than intrinsic to their character. The movement also advanced the idea that individuals with mental illness could recover and reintegrate into society, challenging prevailing beliefs that mental illness was untreatable or incurable. Moral treatment facilities were established as alternatives to the harsh conditions of asylums,

K. Sapp, *Understanding Offending Populations and the Power of Correctional Psychotherapy*, SpringerBriefs in Offending Populations & Correctional Psychotherapy, https://doi.org/10.1007/978-3-031-45886-6_4

implementing practices such as engaging patients in meaningful activities, occupational therapy, and one-on-one interactions with caregivers.

While the Moral Treatment Movement primarily focused on caring for individuals with mental illness, it set a precedent for providing therapeutic interventions within institutional settings. As a result, it influenced the development of correctional psychotherapy by highlighting the importance of compassionate care, individualized treatment, and rehabilitation within correctional settings. Today, the legacy of the Moral Treatment Movement can be seen in contemporary practices that emphasize person-centered care, evidence-based interventions, and the recognition of the inherent dignity and worth of individuals within both mental health and correctional settings.

4.2 Psychodynamic Theories

The emergence of psychodynamic theories in the early twentieth century influenced the understanding and treatment of individuals within the correctional system. Psychodynamic approaches, notably influenced by Sigmund Freud, emphasized the exploration of unconscious conflicts, early life experiences, and defense mechanisms. These theories contributed to recognizing the role of underlying psychological factors in criminal behavior and set the stage for incorporating psychotherapeutic interventions within correctional contexts (Cullen et al., 2011). While the correctional system traditionally focuses on punishment and containment, incorporating psychodynamic principles has underscored the importance of understanding the underlying psychological factors contributing to criminal behaviors and recidivism.

Psychodynamic theories have influenced treatment in the correctional system in several ways:

1. Understanding the underlying psychological factors: Psychodynamic theories emphasize that unconscious conflicts, unresolved trauma, and early life experiences can influence criminal behavior. Integrating psychodynamic principles helps clinicians and therapists in the correctional system understand the deeper psychological factors contributing to criminal behavior (Ward & Beech, 2006). This understanding is essential for developing treatment strategies that address the root causes of offenders' behaviors.
2. Individualized treatment planning: Psychodynamic theories highlight the importance of recognizing and addressing individual offenders' unique needs and experiences within the correctional system. Adapting treatment approaches based on psychodynamic principles allows for a tailored, individualized approach that considers each offender's specific psychological dynamics and history (Clarke, 2011).
3. Exploration of unconscious processes: Incorporating psychodynamic principles encourages the exploration of the unconscious processes and motivations that underlie criminal behavior. By helping offenders gain insight into their

unconscious drives, conflicts, and defense mechanisms, psychodynamic-informed treatment helps identify and address the psychological factors contributing to criminality (Neal & Brodsky, 2012).

4. Therapeutic alliance and transference work: Psychodynamic theories emphasize the therapeutic alliance and the importance of the therapeutic relationship. Within the correctional system, therapists can use the therapeutic relationship to explore and work through transference dynamics, where individuals project unresolved feelings and attitudes onto the therapist. This approach enhances self-awareness, addresses emotional patterns, and promotes personal growth and change (Ward & Beech, 2006).
5. Trauma-informed approach: Psychodynamic theories recognize the impact of early life trauma on individuals' psychological well-being. Applying a trauma-informed approach within the correctional system acknowledges the prevalence of trauma among offenders and integrates psychodynamic principles to address and heal from the effects of trauma (Clarke, 2011).

4.3 Behaviorism and Operant Conditioning

In the mid-twentieth century, behaviorism, particularly the work of B.F. Skinner, had a significant impact on correctional interventions. Skinner's operant conditioning and behavior modification principles provided a framework for modifying behaviors, reducing recidivism, and promoting positive reinforcement within correctional settings. Behaviorist approaches influenced the development of various behavior-oriented programs and interventions to promote prosocial behaviors and reduce deviant behavior (Andrews & Bonta, 2010).

Skinner's theory of operant conditioning focuses on the relationship between behavior and its consequences. According to Skinner, behavior that is reinforced tends to be repeated, while behavior that is not reinforced or is punished is less likely to occur in the future. This fundamental principle formed the basis for Skinner's interventions in the correctional setting.

Skinner's principles have been widely applied in correctional institutions through behavioral modification programs. These programs use positive reinforcement, negative reinforcement, punishment, and extinction to shape desired behaviors and reduce undesired behaviors among offenders (Labott & Ricciardelli, 1988). Through these techniques, behavior modification programs aim to promote prosocial behaviors, increase compliance with rules, and reduce recidivism rates.

One significant application of Skinner's principles in correctional settings is using token economy systems. Token economy programs utilize operant conditioning techniques to reinforce positive behaviors by providing tokens or points that can be exchanged for tangible rewards, such as privileges or desired items (Ayres et al., 2017). These systems have been proven effective in promoting positive behavior change and reducing problem behaviors among incarcerated individuals.

Skinner's principles inform interventions to teach new skills and promote behavior change among offenders. These interventions focus on developing essential prosocial skills, such as anger management, communication, problem-solving, and conflict resolution. By utilizing operant conditioning techniques, these programs encourage the acquisition and maintenance of desirable behaviors while reducing the prevalence of antisocial behaviors (Skinner, 1974).

Skinner's principles have influenced the implementation of contingency management techniques in correctional interventions. Contingency management programs establish contingencies between behavior and consequences, often using rewards or privileges as positive reinforcement for desirable behavior (Warden et al., 2009). These programs reinforce prosocial behaviors and compliance with treatment, reducing the likelihood of recidivism.

The effectiveness of Skinner's influence on correctional interventions has been researched and evaluated. Through empirical studies and meta-analyses, the impact of behavioral programs based on Skinner's principles has been assessed for their ability to reduce recidivism rates and promote positive behavior change among offenders (Mitchell et al., 2012). These evaluations provide empirical evidence supporting the effectiveness of Skinner's principles in shaping behavior within the correctional system.

B.F. Skinner's contributions to the field of correctional interventions, particularly his work on operant conditioning and behaviorism, have profoundly shaped effective treatment strategies within the correctional system. Behavioral modification programs, token economy systems, skill training, and contingency management techniques are among the approaches that can be traced back to Skinner's work. Evidence supports the effectiveness of these interventions in reducing recidivism rates and promoting positive behavior change among offenders.

4.4 Cognitive and Cognitive Behavioral Approaches

In the 1970s, cognitive and cognitive behavioral approaches began to shape correctional psychotherapy practices. Cognitive therapy, pioneered by Aaron Beck, highlighted the role of cognitive distortions and maladaptive thinking patterns in criminal behavior. Since then, cognitive behavioral therapy (CBT) has emerged, combining cognitive restructuring with behavior modification techniques. Cognitive and cognitive behavioral approaches have played a significant role in correctional interventions by addressing cognitive distortions, promoting behavior change, and fostering positive outcomes among individuals in the criminal justice system. These approaches have effectively reduced recidivism rates and enhanced offenders' rehabilitation and reintegration.

A critical role of cognitive and cognitive behavioral approaches in correctional interventions is the identification and modification of cognitive distortions and irrational beliefs that contribute to criminal behavior. Through cognitive restructuring techniques, individuals learn to challenge and replace negative thoughts with more adaptive and rational thinking (Landenberger & Lipsey, 2005). Cognitive and cognitive behavioral interventions emphasize the acquisition of skills that are critical for successful rehabilitation and reintegration. Offenders learn effective communication, anger management, and problem-solving skills. These skill-building techniques enhance their ability to cope with challenges, make positive choices, and address criminogenic needs (Ward et al., 2007).

Cognitive and cognitive behavioral approaches are essential in correctional interventions and promote behavior change. Techniques such as self-monitoring, behavioral activation, and reinforcement of positive behaviors are employed to discourage negative behaviors and foster the development of adaptive behaviors (Ward et al., 2007).

Cognitive and cognitive behavioral approaches target criminogenic needs and factors associated with criminal behavior. These may include substance abuse, antisocial attitudes, and deviant peer associations. By focusing on these needs and addressing them through tailored interventions, cognitive and cognitive behavioral approaches aim to reduce risk factors and enhance protective factors, promoting successful rehabilitation (Landenberger & Lipsey, 2005).

Cognitive and cognitive behavioral interventions empower individuals in correctional settings to take responsibility for their actions and make positive changes in their lives. By fostering self-efficacy, personal responsibility, and accountability, these approaches encourage individuals to actively engage in rehabilitation and develop a sense of agency and control over their behaviors (Ward et al., 2007).

4.5 Trauma-Informed Psychotherapy

Another significant development within correctional psychotherapy is the recognition of the impact of trauma on offending behavior. Trauma-informed approaches emphasize understanding, addressing, and mitigating the effects of trauma in the lives of offenders. This approach acknowledges the complex interaction between trauma, mental health, and criminality, ensuring the provision of safe, sensitive, and effective interventions (Ford & Blaustein, 2013).

Offending populations, including juvenile and adult offenders, often have a high prevalence of trauma exposure due to adverse childhood experiences, victimization, or exposure to violence (Gover & Jennings, 2015). This trauma significantly affects their mental health, coping strategies, and behavioral patterns, contributing to their involvement in the criminal justice system. Trauma-informed psychotherapy holds significant potential for addressing the complex needs of individuals within offending populations who have experienced trauma.

Trauma-informed care emphasizes safety, trustworthiness, choice, collaboration, and empowerment as core principles (Substance Abuse and Mental Health Services Administration [SAMHSA], 2014). In the context of offending populations, these principles underpin the development of therapeutic environments that prioritize safety, respect individuals' experiences, foster collaboration, and facilitate self-empowerment, creating an atmosphere conducive to healing and growth.

Evidence-based interventions have been developed to provide trauma-informed care to offending populations. Trauma-focused cognitive behavioral therapy (TF-CBT) addresses trauma symptoms through cognitive restructuring, skill-building, and trauma narrative work (Cohen et al., 2006). Eye movement desensitization and reprocessing (EMDR) facilitates the processing and integration of traumatic memories (Hogberg et al., 2008). Seeking safety addresses trauma and substance use disorders by focusing on safety and coping skill development (Najavits, 2002).

Trauma-informed psychotherapy in correctional settings has shown promise in reducing recidivism rates among offending populations. By addressing trauma-related factors, such as emotional dysregulation, associated with criminal behavior, trauma-informed interventions contribute to improved behavior management, adaptive coping, and reduced involvement in criminal activities (Green & Wynne, 2004). Implementing trauma-informed psychotherapy in correctional settings requires training and collaboration among correctional staff, mental health professionals, and administrators. Challenges may include limited resources, staff resistance, and systemic barriers. However, overcoming these challenges is crucial to building a supportive environment that fosters trauma-informed care (Ford & Blaustein, 2013). Evaluation studies have demonstrated the effectiveness of trauma-informed psychotherapy in reducing psychological distress, aggression, and recidivism rates among offending populations (Zlotnick et al., 2019). These interventions aid in promoting resilience, improving emotional regulation, and fostering healthier coping mechanisms.

Trauma-informed psychotherapy is pivotal in addressing the psychological needs of offending populations who have experienced trauma. By integrating trauma-informed principles and evidence-based interventions, correctional settings can promote healing, rehabilitation, and reduced recidivism. Recognizing the impact of trauma, implementing trauma-informed care, and fostering collaboration among professionals can facilitate the transformation of correctional environments into spaces of healing, growth, and successful reintegration for these individuals.

4.6 Integration of Evidence-Based Practices

Toward the latter part of the twentieth century and the present, there has been a growing emphasis on integrating evidence-based practices (EBPs) into correctional psychotherapy. Meta-analyses, systematic reviews, and outcome research have contributed to identifying and implementing interventions that effectively reduce recidivism rates and promote positive behavioral change (Andrews et al., 2011). This evidence-based approach has become crucial in shaping the field of correctional psychotherapy.

Integrating evidence-based practice (EBP) into correctional psychotherapy is essential to improve treatment outcomes and promote long-term rehabilitation among individuals in the criminal justice system. This chapter discusses the significance of EBP in correctional settings, explores the benefits of incorporating research findings into treatment approaches, and addresses the challenges and strategies in implementing EBP within correctional psychotherapy.

Evidence-based practice is crucial in guiding treatment decisions and improving outcomes for individuals in the criminal justice system. Research supports the effectiveness of EBP in reducing recidivism rates and enhancing the quality of care provided (Connolly et al., 2019). Integrating research findings into correctional psychotherapy offers several benefits. EBP increases treatment effectiveness, enhances professional credibility, improves transparency, and promotes ethical decision-making (Simpson & Flynn, 2019).

Implementing EBP in correctional settings can present challenges due to limited resources, organizational barriers, and staff resistance to change. However, addressing these challenges is crucial to ensure the delivery of effective interventions (Connolly et al., 2019). Strategies such as staff training and education, collaborative partnerships between researchers and practitioners, and creating a culture of continuous learning have proven effective in overcoming implementation challenges. Supervision and ongoing monitoring are vital to ensure fidelity to evidence-based interventions (Simpson & Flynn, 2019).

Several evidence-based interventions have been successful in correctional settings. Cognitive behavioral therapy (CBT) has effectively reduced recidivism and treated mental health issues among offenders (Landenberger & Lipsey, 2005). Motivational interviewing (MI) has shown promise in addressing substance abuse and facilitating behavior change (Walters, 2017). Evaluation of treatment outcomes is critical to assessing evidence-based interventions' effectiveness in correctional psychotherapy. Regular monitoring and outcome measurement allows for ongoing quality improvement and adjustment of treatment approaches based on empirical evidence (Connolly et al., 2019).

Integrating evidence-based practice into correctional psychotherapy is essential for delivering effective, ethical, and scientifically informed interventions. By incorporating research findings, addressing implementation challenges, and evaluating treatment outcomes, correctional settings can promote meaningful change, reduce recidivism rates, and support the long-term rehabilitation of individuals in the criminal justice system.

4.7 Conclusion

Correctional psychotherapy's early origin and influences can be traced back to various historical and theoretical foundations. The Moral Treatment Movement emphasized humane treatment and therapeutic interventions for individuals in custodial settings. The emergence of psychodynamic theories, behaviorism, and cognitive approaches contributed to understanding mental processes and behavior patterns within correctional contexts. Integrating evidence-based practices has further shaped the field, emphasizing the importance of utilizing interventions that have a proven impact. By understanding and building upon these historical foundations, contemporary correctional psychotherapy continues to evolve, providing effective treatment and rehabilitation within the criminal justice system.

References

Andrews, D. A., & Bonta, J. (2010). *The psychology of criminal conduct* (5th ed.). Routledge.

Andrews, D. A., Bonta, J., & Wormith, J. S. (2011). The recent past and near future of risk and/or need assessment. *Crime & Delinquency, 57*(4), 559–586.

Ayres, M. M., Finney, J. W., Twohey, J. L., & Welte, J. W. (2017). Token economies for substance use treatment: A systematic review. *Journal of Substance Abuse Treatment, 76*, 1–12.

Clarke, J. (2011). *Working with offenders: A guide to concepts and practices*. Jessica Kingsley Publishers.

Cohen, J. A., Mannarino, A. P., & Deblinger, E. (2006). *Treating trauma and traumatic grief in children and adolescents*. Guilford Press.

Connolly, E., Barnert, E. S., & Wilson, L. A. (2019). Addressing mental health and providing evidence-based intervention for justice-involved youth in juvenile justice settings. *Child and Adolescent Psychiatric Clinics, 28*(2), 329–339.

Cullen, F. T., Jonson, C. L., & Bartusch, D. J. (2011). *Correctional criminology: A contemporary overview* (2nd ed.). Routledge.

Ford, J. D., & Blaustein, M. E. (2013). Systemic self-regulation: A framework for trauma-informed services in residential juvenile justice programs. *Journal of Family Violence, 28*(7), 665–677.

Gover, A. R., & Jennings, W. G. (2015). Trauma-informed correctional care: Principles and practices. *American Journal of Public Health, 105*(4), 772–780.

Green, B. L., & Wynne, M. E. (2004). Trauma-informed correctional care: The role of psychologists in addressing the experiences of inmates. *Professional Psychology: Research and Practice, 35*(4), 356–363.

Hogberg, G., Pagani, M., Sundin, O., Soares, J., Aberg-Wistedt, A., Tarnell, B., et al. (2008). Treatment of post-traumatic stress disorder with eye movement desensitization and reprocessing: Outcome is stable in 35-month follow-up. *Psychiatry Research, 159*(1–2), 101–108.

Labott, S. M., & Ricciardelli, R. (1988). Conditioning prison inmates: An application of behavior analysis in a "real world" setting. *Journal of Applied Behavior Analysis, 21*(3), 245–253.

Landenberger, N. A., & Lipsey, M. W. (2005). The positive effects of cognitive-behavioral programs for offenders: A meta-analysis of factors associated with effective treatment. *Journal of Experimental Criminology, 1*(4), 451–476.

Mitchell, O., Wilson, D. B., & MacKenzie, D. L. (2012). The effectiveness of incarceration-based drug treatment on criminal behavior: A systematic review. *Campbell Systematic Reviews, 8*(1), 1–68.

Najavits, L. M. (2002). *Seeking safety: A treatment manual for PTSD and substance abuse*. Guilford Press.

Neal, T. M. S., & Brodsky, S. L. (2012). Approach to psychodynamic treatment of forensic populations. In T. E. Hargrove & E. L. James (Eds.), *Forensic psychology: Research, clinical practice, and applications* (2nd ed., pp. 271–286). Worth Publishers.

Simpson, D. D., & Flynn, P. M. (2019). Moving innovations into treatment: A stage-based approach to program change. *Journal of Substance Abuse Treatment, 96*, 14–25.

Skinner, B. F. (1974). *About behaviorism*. Random House.

Substance Abuse and Mental Health Services Administration. (2014). SAMHSA's concept of trauma and guidance for a trauma-informed approach. SAMHSA.

Walters, S. T. (2017). Motivational interviewing and substance abuse treatment. In W. R. Miller & K. M. Carroll (Eds.), *Rethinking substance abuse: What the science shows, and what we should do about it* (2nd ed., pp. 147–160). The Guilford Press.

Ward, T., & Beech, A. R. (2006). An integrated theory of sexual offending. *Aggression and Violent Behavior, 11*(1), 44–63.

Ward, T., Mann, R. E., & Gannon, T. A. (2007). The good lives model of offender rehabilitation: Clinical implications. *Aggression and Violent Behavior, 12*(1), 87–107.

Warden, D., McGuire, J., Thyer, B. A., & Pfeifer, M. E. (2009). Effects of token reinforcement programs on prison misconduct: A systematic review. *Behavioral Sciences & the Law, 27*(1), 165–186.

Zlotnick, C., Johnson, J., & McCauley, J. (2019). Trauma-informed treatment for justice-involved women. In N. Boyd & L. J. Simpson (Eds.), *Women's mental health: A comprehensive textbook* (2nd ed., pp. 482–494). Oxford University Press.

Chapter 5
Overview of Contemporary Issues in Offending Populations and Correctional Psychotherapy

Correctional psychotherapy is confronted with many contemporary issues among the offending populations within correctional facilities. These individuals face complex challenges that necessitate targeted interventions to address their underlying issues and promote successful rehabilitation, including overcrowding among correctional facilities, limiting access to therapy, and stigma and discrimination. Substance abuse remains a prevalent concern among offenders, with studies indicating high rates of substance use disorders (Daly, 2016; Fazel et al., 2017). Mental health disorders also afflict a significant portion of the offending population, requiring specialized treatment approaches within correctional settings (Binswanger et al., 2010; Skeem et al., 2011). Additionally, the overrepresentation of racial and ethnic minorities within the criminal justice system highlights the need for culturally sensitive correctional psychotherapy (Eitle, 2019; Steffensmeier et al., 2010). Addressing these contemporary issues through evidence-based practices (EBPs) is crucial for effective correctional psychotherapy and reducing recidivism rates.

5.1 Overcrowding in Prisons and Access to Therapy

Prison overcrowding is a pervasive issue affecting correctional systems worldwide, posing significant challenges to delivering therapy services. This section examines the detrimental impacts of prison overcrowding on the accessibility and quality of therapy for inmates. The consequences of overcrowding and associated obstacles to therapy provision within correctional environments are explored by analyzing relevant literature. The effects of prison overcrowding extend beyond the physical limitations of space. Overcrowded prisons strain resources, compromise living conditions, and hinder fulfilling inmates' needs, including access to therapy (Haney, 2003). Moreover, overcrowding exacerbates tension and violence, creating a hostile and stressful prison environment.

K. Sapp, *Understanding Offending Populations and the Power of Correctional Psychotherapy*, SpringerBriefs in Offending Populations & Correctional Psychotherapy, https://doi.org/10.1007/978-3-031-45886-6_5

Overcrowding significantly limits the availability of therapy services in correctional facilities. An overwhelming demand for therapy often surpasses available resources, resulting in long waiting lists for inmates seeking treatment (Metzner & Fellner, 2010). This delay in access to therapy inhibits timely intervention and compromises treatment effectiveness. Overcrowded prisons pressure mental health professionals tremendously, leading to burnout and high turnover rates. The demanding environment and limited resources negatively impact the continuity and quality of therapy services (Metzner & Fellner, 2010). The constant turnover disrupts the establishment of therapeutic rapport, affecting the therapeutic process for inmates.

Overcrowding restricts the implementation of diverse therapeutic modalities in correctional facilities. The lack of space often hinders group therapy, limiting the availability of this practical treatment approach (Haney, 2003). Consequently, the range of evidence-based interventions that benefit inmates is significantly constrained.

Overcrowding directly affects the efficacy of therapy and inmate rehabilitation outcomes. The overcrowded prison environment necessitates shorter or rushed therapy sessions, limiting the comprehensive exploration of underlying issues. This impedes the potential for addressing and resolving inmates' mental health concerns effectively, compromising rehabilitation efforts (Metzner & Fellner, 2010). Inadequate therapy provision may contribute to higher recidivism rates and hinder successful reintegration into society. Furthermore, overcrowded prisons contribute to escalating mental health problems among inmates. The absence of appropriate intervention increases the risk of self-harm, suicidal ideation, and aggression, perpetuating a cycle of psychological distress within the correctional setting (Haney, 2003).

Overcrowding in prisons has significant implications for the accessibility and quality of therapy services provided to inmates, affecting their mental health and rehabilitation prospects. The limited availability of therapy, staff burnout, and restricted treatment modalities pose substantial obstacles within the prison environment. In order to address this critical issue, it is vital to recognize the importance of adequate resources, invest in mental health services, and develop strategies to alleviate overcrowding. Ensuring access to therapy for incarcerated individuals upholds their fundamental rights, promotes overall well-being, and contributes to successful reintegration into society.

5.2 Stigma and Discrimination

Stigma and discrimination are pervasive issues affecting the offending populations within correctional settings. These individuals face not only the challenges of criminal behavior and rehabilitation but also the societal rejection and prejudices that come with their identification as offenders. Correctional psychotherapy plays a crucial role in addressing these contemporary issues by providing support, reducing stigma, and promoting successful reintegration into society. This section delves into the impact of stigma and discrimination on offending populations and the ways in which correctional psychotherapy can mitigate these challenges.

One of the contemporary issues faced by offending populations is the stigmatization they experience due to their criminal history. Stigma refers to the negative attitudes, beliefs, and stereotypes associated with a particular social group (Link & Phelan, 2001). The criminal record of offenders becomes a mark of deviance, making them susceptible to societal rejection and discrimination (Boman & Gallupe, 2016). This stigma can further perpetuate a cycle of recidivism as offenders struggle to find stable housing, employment, and social support upon reintegration into the community (Boman & Gallupe, 2016; Fergusson et al., 2005).

Moreover, discrimination against offending populations exacerbates their already challenging circumstances. Discrimination takes various forms, including limited employment opportunities, housing restrictions, and biased treatment within the criminal justice system (Pager, 2003; Pager & Quillian, 2005). This systemic discrimination hampers the prospects of successful rehabilitation and reintegration, as offenders face significant barriers in accessing resources that are crucial for their recovery (Mauer & Chesney-Lind, 2002).

Correctional psychotherapy interventions are designed to address and mitigate the stigma and discrimination experienced by the offending populations. Through evidence-based approaches such as cognitive behavioral therapy, motivational interviewing, and skills training, correctional psychotherapists aim to tackle the root causes of criminal behavior while promoting prosocial attitudes and behaviors (Andrews & Bonta, 2010a, b). These therapeutic interventions focus on developing empathy, self-awareness, and improving problem-solving skills, which are essential for overcoming societal biases and reducing reoffending (Bonta et al., 2014).

Furthermore, correctional psychotherapy also provides a safe and nonjudgmental space for offenders, where they can explore and address their criminogenic needs and underlying issues. By fostering a therapeutic alliance between therapists and clients, correctional psychotherapy helps to counteract the effects of stigma and discrimination by emphasizing empathy, compassion, and understanding (Belenko, 2006). The therapeutic environment allows for the development of positive relationships, promoting a sense of self-worth and reducing the internalization of negative societal attitudes.

Additionally, correctional psychotherapists play a pivotal role in advocating for the rights and well-being of offenders. They work collaboratively with correctional staff, probation officers, and community organizations to ensure that offenders have access to necessary resources, including education, vocational training, and employment opportunities (Andrews & Bonta, 2010a, b). By addressing systemic barriers and providing comprehensive support services, correctional psychotherapy aims to reduce the impact of stigma and discrimination on the reentry process.

Stigma and discrimination present significant challenges among offending populations that can impede successful rehabilitation and reintegration. Correctional psychotherapy emerges as a vital intervention in combating these contemporary issues, aiming to reduce stigma, promote prosocial attitudes, and advocate for the rights and well-being of offenders. By providing evidence-based therapeutic interventions, creating a safe and inclusive environment, and collaborating with various stakeholders, correctional psychotherapy offers a crucial pathway toward breaking the cycle of stigma and discrimination among the offending populations.

5.2.1 Labeling and Its Impacts

Labeling theory suggests that applying negative labels to individuals can result in a self-fulfilling prophecy, reinforcing criminal behavior and hindering rehabilitation. The process of labeling offenders within the context of correctional settings has significant implications for their identity, perceptions, and future opportunities. Correctional psychotherapy plays a vital role in addressing the impact of labeling on offending populations, working toward reducing the stigma associated with criminality, and promoting successful reintegration into society. This section explores the concept of labeling and its potential consequences among offenders, as well as how correctional psychotherapy can assist in mitigating these impacts.

Labeling theory postulates that individuals who are labeled as deviant, such as "criminal" or "offender," may internalize these labels, leading to a sense of stigmatization and reinforcing criminal behavior (Becker, 1963; Lemert, 1972). Once labeled, individuals may experience difficulties in various aspects, including securing employment, finding housing, and maintaining healthy relationships (Link et al., 1989). The negative perceptions and stereotypes associated with the label "offender" can also lead to social isolation and marginalization, creating barriers to successful reintegration into society.

Furthermore, the labeling process within correctional settings can perpetuate a cycle of criminality. As offenders are continuously exposed to negative labels and treated as members of a deviant group, they may adopt these self-perceptions and engage in further criminal behavior as a response (Braithwaite, 1989). The internalization of the "offender" label can shape their self-concept and reinforce a criminal identity, making it more challenging to break free from the cycle of criminal behavior.

Correctional psychotherapy plays a crucial role in addressing the impact of labeling on offending populations. Through evidence-based interventions, such as cognitive behavioral therapy and strength-based approaches, correctional psychotherapists aim to challenge and reshape the negative self-perceptions and identities associated with the label of "offender" (Andrews & Bonta, 2010a, b; Ward, 2002). By empowering individuals to recognize their strengths, develop prosocial identities, and envision a future beyond their criminal past, correctional psychotherapy aims to counteract the detrimental effects of labeling.

Therapeutic interventions within correctional settings also provide a safe space for individuals to process their experiences and emotions related to the label of "offender." By fostering a therapeutic alliance and offering nonjudgmental support, correctional psychotherapists help offenders develop a more positive self-image and challenge the internalized stigma (Freire, 1996; Lee, 2001). This process can promote a sense of agency and self-worth, enabling individuals to envision a future free from criminality and engage in personal growth.

Moreover, correctional psychotherapy interventions extend beyond individual therapy, including group therapy, peer support programs, and reentry planning. These interventions encourage interpersonal connections, empathy, and shared experiences among individuals labeled as "offenders" (Martin et al., 2013; Solomon, 2011). By fostering a supportive community, correctional psychotherapy helps to counteract the isolation and marginalization often experienced by the offending population, promoting a sense of belonging and encouraging positive behavior change.

Labeling poses significant challenges for the offending populations within correctional settings, influencing their identity, perceptions, and reintegration prospects. Correctional psychotherapy plays a crucial role in mitigating the impact of labeling by providing targeted interventions that challenge negative self-perceptions and foster positive change. By utilizing evidence-based approaches, creating supportive therapeutic environments, and promoting interpersonal connections, correctional psychotherapy aims to empower individuals to overcome the adverse effects of labeling and foster successful rehabilitation and reintegration into society.

5.3 Disproportionate Representation of Marginalized Groups

The disproportionate representation of marginalized groups within the criminal justice system is a pressing contemporary issue with significant implications for correctional psychotherapy. Historically marginalized groups, including racial and ethnic minorities, individuals from lower socioeconomic backgrounds, and those with mental health issues, are overrepresented among the offending populations in correctional settings. This section discusses the causes and consequences of this disproportionate representation and examine how correctional psychotherapy can address the unique challenges these marginalized groups face to foster more equitable and effective rehabilitation.

Racial and ethnic minorities are significantly overrepresented within correctional facilities. Research consistently demonstrates that individuals from these groups are more likely to be arrested, convicted, and incarcerated than their White counterparts (Travis et al., 2014). Similarly, individuals from lower socioeconomic backgrounds, often lacking access to quality education and employment opportunities, are more likely to become entangled in the criminal justice system (Pager, 2007). Moreover, individuals with mental health issues frequently intersect with the criminal justice system, as they may have limited access to appropriate mental health care and are more likely to engage in behaviors that lead to criminalization (Steadman et al., 2009).

The overrepresentation of marginalized groups within the criminal justice system has wide-ranging consequences. Firstly, it perpetuates systemic inequalities and compounds existing in social and economic disparities (Clear, 2007). The adverse effects of incarceration, including limited employment prospects, diminished social support networks, and strained familial relations, disproportionately impact marginalized individuals, contributing to cycles of poverty and criminal recidivism (Western, 2006). Additionally, this disproportionate representation reinforces societal stigmatization and discrimination, further marginalizing individuals upon reentry into their communities (Pager, 2007).

Correctional psychotherapy serves as a critical intervention to address the challenges marginalized groups face in correctional settings. By utilizing culturally responsive treatment approaches, correctional psychotherapy recognizes and addresses these individuals' unique experiences and needs (Andrews & Bonta, 2010a, b). Evidence-based interventions, such as cognitive behavioral therapy and trauma-informed care, can be tailored to consider the cultural and contextual factors impacting marginalized individuals' pathways to offending (Baglivio et al., 2020).

Furthermore, correctional psychotherapy can be pivotal in addressing social determinants of crime and providing comprehensive support. Therapists actively collaborate with correctional staff, community organizations, and social service agencies to develop reentry plans that address housing insecurity, employment barriers, and health disparities (Belenko, 2016; Van Voorhis et al., 2010). Correctional psychotherapy aims to equip marginalized individuals with the necessary resources and skills for successful reintegration into society by facilitating access to education, vocational training, and healthcare.

To promote equitable rehabilitation, correctional psychotherapy must advocate for systemic changes. This involves challenging biased policies, advocating for alternatives to incarceration, and promoting interventions that address the underlying societal factors contributing to the overrepresentation of marginalized groups in the criminal justice system (Braithwaite, 2018; Clear, 2007). By actively engaging stakeholders and drawing attention to systemic injustices, correctional psychotherapy can contribute to broader criminal justice reform efforts and reduce disproportionate representation.

The disproportionate representation of marginalized groups within the criminal justice system poses significant challenges to effective rehabilitation. Correctional psychotherapy, through its culturally responsive approaches, comprehensive support services, and advocacy for systemic change, plays a vital role in addressing the unique needs of these marginalized individuals. By fostering equitable rehabilitation, correctional psychotherapy can contribute to a more just and inclusive society where marginalized individuals have opportunities for rehabilitation and successful reintegration.

5.4 Mental Health, Substance Use, and Addictions

The prevalence of mental health disorders, substance use, and addiction among offending populations is a significant contemporary issue that requires attention in the context of correctional psychotherapy. Individuals within correctional facilities often exhibit complex psychosocial challenges, including high rates of mental health disorders and substance use disorders. Correctional psychotherapy addresses these co-occurring issues, providing evidence-based interventions to help individuals manage their mental health, address substance use, and establish a foundation for successful rehabilitation.

Mental health disorders are prevalent among offending populations, often at higher rates than the general population (Fazel et al., 2016). Conditions such as depression, anxiety disorders, post-traumatic stress disorder, and personality disorders are frequently observed among incarcerated individuals. Contributing factors include adverse childhood experiences, trauma, substance use, poverty, and limited access to mental healthcare services (Fazel et al., 2016; Skeem et al., 2006).

Substance use disorders, including drug and alcohol addiction, are also pervasive among offending populations (Binswanger et al., 2012). Many individuals use substances to cope with their challenging circumstances, leading to a cycle of addiction, criminal behavior, and incarceration (Binswanger et al., 2012; Martin et al., 2014). The lack of access to substance abuse treatment and the social and economic consequences of substance use contributes to the perpetuation of this cycle.

Correctional psychotherapy is critical in addressing the mental health and substance use challenges of offending populations. By offering evidence-based interventions, such as cognitive behavioral therapy and trauma-informed care, correctional psychotherapists work to identify and manage symptoms of mental health disorders, develop coping strategies, and improve overall psychological well-being (Frueh et al., 2017; Skeem et al., 2006). Additionally, correctional psychotherapy provides substance abuse treatment programs, including motivational interviewing, relapse prevention, and harm reduction strategies (Martin et al., 2014). These interventions aim to address the underlying causes of substance use disorders, enhance motivation for change, promote healthy coping mechanisms, and facilitate recovery and relapse prevention. Moreover, correctional psychotherapy can assist in bridging the gap between correctional facilities and community-based mental health and substance abuse treatment programs. By collaborating with community providers, correctional psychotherapists help ensure continuity of care upon release, providing individuals with ongoing support and resources to maintain their mental health and sobriety in the community (van den Berk-Clark et al., 2016).

In conclusion, mental health disorders, substance use, and addiction pose significant challenges to the offending populations within correctional facilities. Correctional psychotherapy emerges as an essential tool in addressing these contemporary issues, providing evidence-based interventions that target mental health symptoms, substance use, and addiction. Through comprehensive therapeutic approaches, collaboration with community providers, and a focus on continuity of care, correctional psychotherapy is crucial in promoting psychological well-being, sobriety, and successful rehabilitation among those involved with the criminal justice system.

5.4.1 *Evidence-Based Practices*

Adopting and implementing evidence-based practices (EBPs) within correctional psychotherapy are essential contemporary issues for addressing the complex needs of offending populations. EBPs refer to therapeutic interventions and approaches that have been extensively researched and proven effective through rigorous scientific studies. By integrating EBPs into correctional psychotherapy, practitioners can provide high-quality, research-informed treatment, leading to improved outcomes and successful rehabilitation. This section examines the significance of EBPs, their benefits, and the challenges associated with their implementation in correctional settings.

The significance of EBPs lies in their ability to guide intervention approaches grounded in research that has demonstrated positive outcomes among offending populations. By utilizing interventions that have proven effectiveness, correctional psychotherapy can enhance treatment success, reduce recidivism rates, and improve overall well-being for individuals within correctional settings (Andrews & Bonta, 2010a, b; Taxman, 2014). EBPs provide a framework for correctional practitioners to deliver targeted interventions and utilize best practices that align with the specific needs of offenders.

The incorporation of EBPs into correctional psychotherapy offers several benefits. Firstly, EBPs increase treatment effectiveness by ensuring interventions are based on empirical evidence rather than relying solely on intuition or anecdotal experience (Palmer et al., 2018). Practitioners increase the likelihood of positive treatment outcomes by utilizing strategies and techniques that have proven successful in reducing targeted behaviors or symptoms.

Additionally, EBPs help standardize treatment practices within correctional settings. This consistency ensures that individuals receive equitable access to evidence-based interventions, regardless of their location within the correctional system (Andrews & Bonta, 2010a, b). Standardization also allows for collecting reliable data on treatment efficacy and provides ongoing improvement and quality assurance opportunities.

Despite the many advantages of EBPs, their implementation within correctional settings poses challenges. One challenge relates to resource availability. Limited funding, staff shortages, and logistical constraints can impede providing training and ongoing support to correctional staff to deliver EBPs (Houser et al., 2020). Moreover, the hierarchical culture within corrections may present barriers to adopting new practices and engaging staff in training initiatives (Houser et al., 2020).

Another challenge involves the cultural and contextual considerations specific to the correctional environment. Adapting EBPs to the unique needs and challenges of individuals within the criminal justice system, such as addressing issues related to trauma, substance use, and antisocial behaviors, requires thoughtful implementation and tailoring (Lehmann et al., 2019). Overcoming these challenges requires collaboration among correctional administrators, policymakers, and researchers to develop sustainable strategies for EBP implementation and support (Palmer et al., 2018). Investment in staff training, ongoing supervision, and continuous improvement culture is crucial for successfully integrating EBPs within correctional psychotherapy (Lehmann et al., 2019).

In conclusion, evidence-based practices offer considerable potential for enhancing the effectiveness of correctional psychotherapy and promoting successful rehabilitation among offending populations. By basing treatment approaches on research evidence, practitioners can provide equitable and targeted interventions that address individuals' particular needs and challenges within correctional settings. While challenges exist, committing to ongoing staff training and resource allocation and adapting EBPs to the correctional context can successfully integrate evidence-based practices in correctional psychotherapy, leading to improved outcomes for offenders and increased public safety.

5.4.2 Trauma-Informed Care

The prevalence of trauma among offending populations within correctional settings is a critical contemporary issue that necessitates a trauma-informed approach in correctional psychotherapy. Many individuals within the criminal justice system have experienced significant trauma, which often underlies their criminal behavior. Trauma-informed care recognizes the impact of trauma and aims to provide supportive, empowering, and healing interventions.

Trauma-informed care recognizes the traumatic experiences that individuals may have faced, such as physical abuse, sexual assault, neglect, or exposure to violence. It acknowledges that trauma can profoundly affect individuals' mental health, emotions, behaviors, and overall well-being. By integrating trauma-informed principles into correctional psychotherapy, practitioners can create an environment that promotes safety, trust, and empowerment, facilitating healing and resilience.

Implementing trauma-informed care within correctional psychotherapy offers numerous benefits. Firstly, it fosters a culture of safety and trust, essential in establishing therapeutic relationships with individuals who have experienced trauma (Harris, 2019). By promoting safety, practitioners increase the likelihood of engagement and collaboration, enabling individuals to explore their traumatic experiences within a supportive environment. Secondly, trauma-informed care acknowledges the complex intersections between trauma, mental health, and substance use disorders often observed among the offending populations (Harris, 2019; Najavits, 2015). Practitioners provide interventions that address the underlying trauma-related symptoms, such as flashbacks, hypervigilance, and emotional dysregulation, allowing individuals to develop healthy coping strategies and reduce self-destructive behaviors. Moreover, trauma-informed care emphasizes a strength-based approach, focusing on individual resilience rather than pathology (Harris, 2019). This approach supports individuals in recognizing their inherent strengths, promoting self-efficacy and positive identity formation, ultimately aiding in their rehabilitation and successful reintegration into society.

Implementing trauma-informed care within correctional settings presents challenges. One challenge involves comprehensive training and education for correctional staff to understand trauma's impact and develop skills to create safe and therapeutic environments (Harris, 2019; Najavits, 2015). Training initiatives must address the trauma histories of staff and offenders to ensure sensitivity, awareness, and appropriate responses. Additionally, resource constraints and the structural limitations of correctional settings may hinder the implementation of trauma-informed care (McKenna et al., 2019). Adequate staffing levels, physical environments conducive to healing, and access to specialized trauma-focused interventions can be significant logistical challenges. Overcoming these challenges requires organizational commitment and systemic changes within correctional settings. This involves implementing trauma-informed policies, fostering culture, and allocating resources for training and trauma-focused interventions (Harris, 2019; McKenna et al., 2019).

Trauma-informed care is paramount in addressing the significant trauma experienced by the offending populations within correctional settings. By applying trauma-informed principles, correctional psychotherapy can create safe, empowering, and healing environments that acknowledge the impact of trauma on individuals' lives. The benefits of trauma-informed care, including a culture of safety, addressing trauma-related symptoms, and emphasizing strengths, contribute to successful rehabilitation and reintegration. While challenges exist, a commitment to training, system-level changes, and resource allocation can facilitate the implementation of trauma-informed care, leading to improved outcomes for individuals involved in the criminal justice system.

5.4.3 Cultural Sensitivity

Cultural sensitivity is a significant contemporary issue in correctional psychotherapy when working with offending populations. The diverse backgrounds of individuals within correctional settings necessitate a culturally sensitive approach to providing effective and equitable treatment. Cultural sensitivity recognizes and respects individuals' various values, beliefs, customs, and experiences, considering how culture influences their behaviors, perceptions, and responses to treatment. This section explores the significance of cultural sensitivity, its benefits, and the challenges in implementing this approach within correctional settings.

Given the diversity among offending populations, cultural sensitivity is crucial within correctional psychotherapy. Individuals come from various racial, ethnic, and cultural backgrounds, each with unique perspectives and experiences. Incorporating cultural sensitivity into therapeutic interventions helps ensure that treatment is appropriate, effective, and respectful of the individuals' cultural identities. By valuing diversity and cultural differences, correctional psychotherapy can reduce disparities, enhance engagement, and provide more equitable treatment outcomes.

Implementing cultural sensitivity within correctional psychotherapy offers several benefits. Firstly, it enhances rapport and trust between practitioners and individuals by demonstrating respect for their cultural backgrounds (Constantine & Sue, 2006). By acknowledging and valuing cultural diversity, practitioners foster a therapeutic alliance that encourages open communication and engagement in treatment. Secondly, cultural sensitivity acknowledges the influence of culture on individuals' behaviors, beliefs, and help-seeking preferences (American Psychological Association, 2017). It allows practitioners to tailor treatment approaches, considering individuals' cultural values and traditions and incorporating them into therapeutic interventions. This alignment between treatment and cultural values increases the relevance and acceptability of interventions, leading to improved treatment engagement and outcomes.

Moreover, cultural sensitivity promotes equity in treatment by addressing disparities arising from cultural biases and systemic inequalities (Bernal & Domenech Rodríguez, 2012). By being aware of cultural factors, practitioners can identify and mitigate barriers to treatment, such as language barriers, stigma, or lack of cultural understanding. This approach ensures that individuals from diverse cultural backgrounds have equal access to quality care and are not disadvantaged due to cultural differences.

Implementing cultural sensitivity within correctional settings presents challenges. One challenge lies in developing practitioners' cultural competence through education, training, and self-reflection (Sue, 2006). It requires practitioners to actively engage in learning about diverse cultures, examine their biases, and reflect on their cultural beliefs and values. Additionally, the correctional environment may have limitations that impact the implementation of cultural sensitivity, such as limited resources or restrictive policies (American Psychological Association, 2017). These limitations can hinder the provision of culturally appropriate interventions and specialized services. Overcoming these challenges requires cultural competence at both individual and organizational levels. Training initiatives should focus on increasing practitioners' understanding of diverse cultures, providing opportunities for self-reflection and examination of biases, and encouraging ongoing professional development (Bernal & Domenech Rodríguez, 2012). Administrators should also promote a culture of inclusivity, diversity, and cultural responsiveness, ensuring that correctional policies and practices support cultural sensitivity.

Cultural sensitivity is pivotal in correctional psychotherapy when working with diverse offending populations. Correctional psychotherapy can provide effective and equitable treatment by valuing and integrating individuals' cultural backgrounds. Benefits include improved rapport, treatment engagement, and treatment outcomes. Despite challenges, a commitment to cultural competence, ongoing training, and organizational support can help practitioners implement cultural sensitivity within correctional settings, ultimately striving for more inclusive and effective interventions.

5.5 Reintegration and Rehabilitation

Reintegration and rehabilitation of individuals within offending populations are critical contemporary issues that require attention in the context of correctional psychotherapy. The successful reintegration of offenders into society has far-reaching implications for reducing recidivism rates, promoting public safety, and facilitating individual well-being. Correctional psychotherapy plays a vital role in addressing the complex needs of this population, providing evidence-based interventions to facilitate reintegration and promote rehabilitation.

Reintegration and rehabilitation are crucial in addressing the complex challenges faced by individuals within offending populations. Incarceration alone does not address the underlying causes of criminal behavior or equip individuals with the necessary skills to lead productive, law-abiding lives upon release (Andrews & Bonta, 2010a, b). Reintegration and rehabilitation aim to provide offenders with the tools, support, and opportunities needed to break the patterns of criminal behavior, rebuild their lives, and contribute positively to society.

Correctional psychotherapy offers several benefits for reintegration and rehabilitation. Firstly, evidence-based interventions delivered within correctional settings help individuals address underlying issues such as substance abuse, mental health disorders, and distorted thinking patterns contributing to criminal behavior (Andrews & Bonta, 2010a, b). By targeting these criminogenic needs, psychotherapy promotes behavior change, reduces the risk of recidivism, and enhances overall well-being. Secondly, correctional psychotherapy assists individuals in developing essential skills for successful reintegration, such as problem-solving, communication, anger management, and interpersonal skills (Andrews & Bonta, 2010a, b). These interventions provide individuals with the tools to navigate challenges, build positive relationships, secure employment, and become productive members of society upon release. Moreover, correctional psychotherapy enhances the individuals' self-awareness, emotional regulation, and empathy through therapeutic interventions such as cognitive behavioral therapy, trauma-focused therapy, and psychosocial education (LaVelle et al., 2020). By fostering personal growth, improving psychological well-being, and promoting prosocial values, correctional psychotherapy supports individuals in transforming their identities and making positive behavioral changes.

Successful reintegration faces challenges that can impede individuals' ability to reintegrate effectively into society. Structural barriers, such as limited access to housing, education, employment, and social support, can hinder individuals' prospects for successful reintegration (Travis, 2005). Negative social attitudes and stigma toward former offenders can exacerbate these challenges, making it difficult for individuals to secure stable employment or rebuild relationships with family and community members (Pager, 2003). Furthermore, a lack of coordination and continuity of care between correctional facilities and community-based support services can disrupt individuals' access to necessary resources upon release (Andrews & Bonta, 2010a, b). Inadequate transitional planning and support may lead to service gaps, leaving individuals at higher risk for relapse and reoffending. To address these challenges, integrated reentry programs that provide comprehensive support, continuity of care, and collaboration among correctional institutions, community organizations, and support networks are essential (LaVelle et al., 2020). By addressing structural barriers and providing ongoing support during the reentry process, successful reintegration can be facilitated.

Ultimately, reintegration and rehabilitation are crucial contemporary issues within the context of offending populations. Correctional psychotherapy plays a vital role in addressing these issues by providing evidence-based interventions, teaching essential skills, promoting personal growth, and supporting individuals in their journey toward successful reintegration. Correctional psychotherapy reduces recidivism rates by mitigating the challenges individuals face during reentry, such as structural barriers and social stigma. It improves community safety and the overall well-being of formerly incarcerated individuals.

5.6 Restorative Justice

Restorative justice is a significant contemporary issue in correctional psychotherapy for offending populations. Recognizing the limitations of punitive approaches, restorative justice addresses the harm caused by crime by focusing on repairing the damage, facilitating healing, and promoting accountability for all parties involved. Furthermore, restorative justice provides an alternative framework prioritizing recovery, community involvement, and rehabilitation. By shifting the focus away from punishment alone, restorative justice recognizes the humanity of all stakeholders and seeks to repair harm while promoting accountability and transforming relationships (Zehr, 2002). This approach can address systemic barriers to successful reintegration and reduce recidivism rates, leading to more balanced and meaningful outcomes for both offenders and victims.

Restorative justice offers several benefits when integrated into correctional psychotherapy. Firstly, it provides an opportunity for offenders to take responsibility for their actions, understand the impact of their actions on others, and actively contribute to the healing process (Braithwaite, 2002). This increased sense of agency and engagement promotes an internal drive for behavioral change and reduces the likelihood of reoffending. Secondly, restorative justice facilitates dialogue and understanding between offenders, victims, and the broader community. Involving all parties in the process promotes empathy, fosters communication, and supports victim healing (Wachtel & McCold, 2000). This engagement offers a chance for victims to receive validation, closure, and a sense of justice while allowing offenders to develop empathy and reconnect with the human consequences of their actions.

Moreover, restorative justice focuses on repairing harm and addressing the underlying causes of criminal behavior. It emphasizes rehabilitation and reintegrating offenders into the community as productive, law-abiding citizens (Umbreit & Coates, 1993). By providing opportunities for personal growth, skill development, and community involvement, restorative justice aligns closely with the goals of correctional psychotherapy in promoting successful rehabilitation.

Implementing restorative justice within correctional settings presents challenges. One challenge involves fostering a culture that embraces restorative principles and practices. This requires a shift in attitudes and perceptions among correctional staff, the judiciary, and the general public, as restorative justice diverges from traditional punitive approaches (Latimer et al., 2005). Additionally, ensuring accessible and meaningful restorative processes for all parties can be challenging. Victims may face barriers to participation, such as fear, trauma, or lack of support. Offenders must also be willing and able to actively engage in the restorative process (Umbreit, 2001). Addressing power imbalances, providing adequate support, and ensuring a safe and inclusive environment for all participants are critical considerations in implementing restorative justice effectively.

Restorative justice is a significant contemporary issue in correctional psychotherapy working with offending populations. Restorative justice offers a promising alternative to punitive approaches within correctional systems by prioritizing healing, accountability, and community engagement. Its benefits, including promoting personal growth, repairing harm, and fostering community reintegration, align closely with the goals of correctional psychotherapy. Despite challenges in implementation, a shift toward restorative justice can contribute to more meaningful and effective rehabilitation outcomes for offenders and society.

5.7 Conclusion

Addressing contemporary issues among offending populations is crucial within correctional psychotherapy. This chapter provides a comprehensive definition of various offending populations within the criminal justice system and begun examining the historical context of correctional psychotherapy. Furthermore, this chapter explores several significant contemporary issues, including stigma and discrimination, disproportionate representation of marginalized groups, trauma, substance use and addiction, evidence-based practices, cultural sensitivity, and reintegration and rehabilitation.

Correctional psychotherapy, with its evidence-based interventions and person-centered approaches, addresses these challenges and promotes successful rehabilitation. By adopting evidence-based practices, correctional psychotherapy offers interventions grounded in research and proven efficacy in addressing the complex needs of offenders. Integrating trauma-informed care and cultural sensitivity ensures that therapy is respectful, relevant, and effective in supporting individuals who have experienced trauma and come from diverse backgrounds. Additionally, therapeutic justice approaches provide opportunities for healing, accountability, and community involvement, fostering a more holistic approach to rehabilitation. However, these contemporary issues still face their challenges. Limited resources, structural barriers, biases, and lack of coordination can hinder the implementation of effective interventions. Overcoming these challenges requires a commitment to ongoing training, organizational support, collaboration among stakeholders, and systemic changes within the correctional system.

In conclusion, addressing contemporary issues among offending populations requires a multidimensional approach that prioritizes evidence-based interventions, trauma-informed care, cultural sensitivity, and restorative justice practices. Correctional psychotherapy is crucial in promoting successful rehabilitation, reducing recidivism rates, and empowering individuals to reintegrate into society as productive, law-abiding citizens. By actively addressing these contemporary issues, we ensure that correctional systems prioritize holistic well-being, equity, and social justice for all individuals involved.

References

American Psychological Association. (2017). *Multicultural guidelines: An ecological approach to context, identity, and intersectionality*. Retrieved from https://www.apa.org/about/policy/multicultural-guidelines.pdf

Andrews, D. A., & Bonta, J. (2010a). *The psychology of criminal conduct* (5th ed.). Routledge.

Andrews, D. A., & Bonta, J. (2010b). Rehabilitating criminal justice policy and practice. *Psychology, Public Policy, and Law, 16*(1), 39–55.

Baglivio, M. T., Wolff, K. T., DeLisi, M., & Jackowski, K. (2020). The Role of Adverse Childhood Experiences (ACEs) and Psychopathic Features on Juvenile Offending Criminal Careers to Age 18. *Youth Violence and Juvenile Justice, 18*(4), 337–364. https://doi.org/10.1177/1541204020927075

Becker, H. S. (1963). *Outsiders: Studies in the sociology of deviance*. Free Press.

Belenko, S. (2006). Research on drug courts: A critical review 2001 update. *National Drug Court Institute Review, 3*(1), 1–47.

Belenko, S. (2016). Addressing substance abuse treatment needs of incarcerated adults: The role of the criminal justice system. In J. M. Blanco, K. S. Bolla, & R. G. Cullom (Eds.), *Alcohol, drugs, and criminality in American society* (pp. 147–161). Springer.

Bernal, G., & Domenech Rodríguez, M. M. (2012). Cultural adaptation in context: Psychotherapy para Latinos. *Journal of Clinical Psychology: In Session, 68*(4), 493–503.

Binswanger, I. A., Blatchford, P. J., Mueller, S. R., & Stern, M. F. (2010). Mortality after prison release: Opioid overdose and other causes of death, risk factors, and time trends from 1999 to 2009. *Annals of Internal Medicine, 152*(3), 175–183.

Binswanger, I. A., Blatchford, P. J., Lindsay, R. G., & Stern, M. F. (2012). Risk factors for all cause, overdose and early deaths after release from prison in Washington state. *Drug and Alcohol Dependence, 123*(1–3), 19–25.

Boman, J. H., & Gallupe, O. (2016). Public support for punishment and rehabilitation: Stigma, perceived severity, and deservingness. *Criminal Justice and Behavior, 43*(10), 1316–1338.

Bonta, J., Blais, J., & Wilson, H. A. (2014). A theoretically informed meta-analysis of the risk for general and violent recidivism for mentally disordered offenders. *Aggression and Violent Behavior, 19*(3), 278–287.

Braithwaite, J. (1989). *Crime, shame, and reintegration*. Cambridge University Press.

Braithwaite, J. (2002). *Restorative justice and responsive regulation*. Oxford University Press.

Braithwaite, J. (2018). *Restorative justice: A contemporary perspective* (3rd ed.). Routledge.

Clear, T. R. (2007). The effects of high imprisonment rates on communities. *Crime and Justice, 34*(1), 97–132.

Constantine, M. G., & Sue, D. W. (2006). Factors contributing to optimal human functioning in people of color in the United States. *The Counseling Psychologist, 34*(2), 228–244.

Daly, C. (2016). *Prevalence of mental health and addiction in adult and youth correctional facilities: A literature review*. Correctional Service of Canada.

Eitle, D. J. (2019). Incarceration and racial/ethnic disparities among drug-involved offenders. *Journal of Drug Issues, 49*(3), 459–480.

Fazel, S., Seewald, K., & Severe, J. B. (2016). Mental health of prisoners: Prevalence, adverse outcomes, and interventions. *The Lancet Psychiatry, 3*(9), 871–881.

Fazel, S., Hayes, A. J., Bartellas, K., Clerici, M., & Trestman, R. (2017). Mental health of prisoners: Prevalence, adverse outcomes, and interventions. *The Lancet Psychiatry, 4*(9), 749–761.

Fergusson, D. M., Swain-Campbell, N., Moffitt, T. E., & Caspi, A. (2005). Assessing child maltreatment frequency and severity as predictors of early adulthood outcomes: The Dunedin Multidisciplinary Health and Development Study. *Child Abuse & Neglect, 29*(7), 749–768.

Freire, P. (1996). *Pedagogy of the oppressed* (Revised ed.). Continuum.

Frueh, B. C., Knapp, R. G., Cusack, K. J., Grubaugh, A. L., Sauvageot, J. A., Cousins, V. C., et al. (2017). Patients' report of traumatic or harmful experiences within the psychiatric setting. *Psychiatric Services, 58*(7), 830–835.

Haney, C. (2003). Mental health issues in long-term solitary and "supermax" confinement. *Crime and Delinquency, 49*(1), 124–156.

Harris, M. (2019). Healing-centered corrections: A framework for trauma-informed practice with justice-involved individuals. *Health & Social Work, 44*(4), 223–226.

Houser, K. A., Belenko, S., & Brennan, P. K. (2020). Implementation of evidence-based practices within the criminal justice system: Challenges, barriers, and recommendations. *Journal of Offender Rehabilitation, 59*(2), 136–155.

Latimer, J., Dowden, C., & Muise, D. (2005). The effectiveness of restorative justice practices: A meta-analysis. *The Prison Journal, 85*(2), 127–144.

LaVelle, M., Trestman, R. L., Benner, K., & Metzner, J. (2020). Correctional psychiatry: A new paradigm for comprehensive prevention and intervention. *American Journal of Psychiatry, 177*(1), 6–10.

Lee, H. C. (2001). The effect of self-stigma on the recovery of people with schizophrenia: A longitudinal study. *Asian Journal of Psychiatry, 4*(3), 143–147.

Lehmann, P., Ristenpart, E., & Myers, R. S. (2019). Mass customization of treatment in a prison based substance use disorder program: Implementation of an evidence-based practice. *Journal of Offender Rehabilitation, 58*(5), 303–321.

Lemert, E. M. (1972). *Human deviance, social problems, and social control* (2nd ed.). Prentice Hall.

Link, B. G., & Phelan, J. C. (2001). Conceptualizing stigma. *Annual Review of Sociology, 27*(1), 363–385.

Link, B. G., Cullen, F. T., Struening, E., Shrout, P. E., & Dohrenwend, B. P. (1989). A modified labeling theory approach to mental disorders: An empirical assessment. *American Sociological Review, 54*(3), 400–423.

Martin, M. S., Butzin, C. A., & Inciardi, J. A. (2013). Assessment and treatment of prison inmates with substance use disorders. *Rehabilitation Research and Practice, 2013*, 1–10.

Martin, A. E., Young, C., Edens, J. F., & Skeem, J. (2014). The ability of mental health and substance use screens to predict recidivism among offenders is related to recidivism prevalence. *Psychological Services, 11*(4), 441–453.

Mauer, M., & Chesney-Lind, M. (2002). *Invisible punishment: The collateral consequences of mass imprisonment*. The New Press.

McKenna, R., Watson, B. L., Myers, D., Conway, C., Baughman, S., & McCollister, K. (2019). Implementing trauma-informed care in correctional settings: Key components, processes, and lessons learned. *Journal of Correctional Health Care, 25*(3), 236–250.

Metzner, J. L., & Fellner, J. (2010). Solitary confinement and mental illness in U.S. prisons: A challenge for medical ethics. *The Journal of the American Academy of Psychiatry and the Law, 38*(1), 104–108.

Najavits, L. M. (2015). *Trauma-informed care in criminal justice*. American Psychological Association.
Pager, D. (2003). The mark of a criminal record. *American Journal of Sociology, 108*(5), 937–975.
Pager, D. (2007). *Marked: Race, crime, and finding work in an era of mass incarceration*. University of Chicago Press.
Pager, D., & Quillian, L. (2005). Walking the talk? What employers say versus what they do. *American Sociological Review, 70*(3), 355–380.
Palmer, E., Kavish, N., & Hoyt, W. T. (2018). Facilitating evidence-based treatment implementation in correctional settings: A systematic review and meta-analysis. *Journal of Offender Rehabilitation, 57*(2), 149–172.
Skeem, J. L., Manchak, S., & Peterson, J. K. (2006). Correctional policy for offenders with mental illness: Creating a new paradigm for recidivism reduction. *Law and Human Behavior, 30*(1), 1–21.
Skeem, J. L., Manchak, S., & Peterson, J. K. (2011). Correctional policy for offenders with mental illness: Creating a new paradigm for recidivism reduction. *Law and Human Behavior, 35*(2), 110–126.
Solomon, P. (2011). Peer support/peer provided services: Underlying processes, benefits, and critical ingredients. *Psychiatric Rehabilitation Journal, 35*(1), 9–14.
Steadman, H. J., Osher, F. C., Robbins, P. C., Case, B., & Samuels, S. (2009). Prevalence of serious mental illness among jail inmates. *Psychiatric Services, 60*(6), 761–765.
Steffensmeier, D. J., Ulmer, J. T., & Kramer, J. H. (2010). The interaction of race, gender, and age in criminal sentencing: The punishment cost of being young, black, and male. *Criminology, 48*(1), 281–323.
Sue, D. W. (2006). Cultural competence matters in all of psychology. *American Psychologist, 61*(6), 518–526.
Taxman, F. S. (2014). Treating adult substance abuse using technology-based interventions in criminal justice settings. *Research on Social Work Practice, 24*(1), 11–19.
Travis, J. (2005). *But they all come back: Facing the challenges of prisoner reentry*. Urban Institute Press.
Travis, J., Western, B., & Redburn, F. S. (2014). *The growth of incarceration in the United States: Exploring causes and consequences*. National Academies Press.
Umbreit, M. S. (2001). Victim meets offender: The impact of restorative justice and mediation. *Criminal Justice and Behavior, 28*(5), 567–598.
Umbreit, M. S., & Coates, R. B. (1993). *Handbook of restorative justice*. Routledge.
van den Berk-Clark, C., McGuire, J., Witt, S., & Gilchrist, L. (2016). Resilience in incarcerated adults: A dependent variable approach. *Traumatology, 22*(1), 37–45.
Van Voorhis, P., Wright, E. M., Salisbury, E., & Bauman, A. (2010). Women's risk factors and their contributions to existing risk/needs assessment: The current status of a gender-responsive supplement. *Criminal Justice and Behavior, 37*(3), 261–288.
Wachtel, T., & McCold, P. (2000). Restorative justice in everyday life. In E. Weitekamp & H.-J. Kerner (Eds.), *Restorative justice in context: International practice and directions*. Dartmouth Publishing.
Ward, T. (2002). The good lives model and its application to practice. *Sexual Abuse: A Journal of Research and Treatment, 14*(2), 95–105.
Western, B. (2006). *Punishment and inequality in America*. Russell Sage Foundation.
Zehr, H. (2002). *The little book of restorative justice*. Good Books.

Chapter 6
Offender Rehabilitation as a Contemporary Issue

Offender rehabilitation is a critical contemporary issue within the realm of criminal justice. With a growing understanding that punitive approaches alone are insufficient in reducing recidivism and promoting public safety, the focus has shifted toward evidence-based practices (EBPs) and holistic interventions aimed at rehabilitating individuals who have engaged in criminal behavior. This chapter explores the significance of offender rehabilitation as a contemporary issue, the underlying principles and approaches, and the challenges and opportunities in implementing effective rehabilitation programs.

The significance of offender rehabilitation lies in its potential to break the cycle of criminal behavior, promote successful reintegration into society, and contribute to safer communities. Traditional punitive measures alone often fail to address the underlying causes of criminal behavior, such as substance abuse, mental health issues, lack of education, and limited employment prospects (Andrews & Bonta, 2010). By focusing on rehabilitation, however, the criminal justice system can address these complex needs and target the factors that contribute to offending, thereby reducing recidivism rates and improving public safety.

Effective offender rehabilitation is grounded in evidence-based principles and approaches. These principles emphasize individualized treatment plans, risk and needs assessment, cognitive behavioral interventions, and the use of therapeutic techniques that promote positive behavioral change (Andrews & Bonta, 2010). Approaches such as cognitive behavioral therapy (CBT), vocational training, substance abuse counseling, and education programs have shown promise in addressing criminogenic factors and promoting successful reintegration (Taxman, 2018).

Implementing effective rehabilitation programs poses challenges within the criminal justice system. Limited resources, organizational resistance, systemic barriers, and a punitive-oriented culture can hinder the implementation of evidence-based approaches (Taxman, 2018). Additionally, ensuring continuity of care and providing support during the reentry process are essential for successful

K. Sapp, *Understanding Offending Populations and the Power of Correctional Psychotherapy*, SpringerBriefs in Offending Populations & Correctional Psychotherapy, https://doi.org/10.1007/978-3-031-45886-6_6

rehabilitation (Andrews & Bonta, 2010). However, these challenges present opportunities for collaboration among stakeholders, policy reforms, training initiatives, and the integration of community-based resources (Taxman, 2018).

6.1 Key Concepts in Offender Rehabilitation

Offender rehabilitation is a dynamic and multifaceted process that aims to reduce recidivism, promote positive change, and facilitate the successful reintegration of individuals involved in criminal behavior. This section examines key concepts in offender rehabilitation, including individualized treatment, evidence-based practices, continuous support, and collaboration between criminal justice agencies and community organizations. Understanding these concepts is vital for designing and implementing effective rehabilitation programs within the criminal justice system.

6.1.1 Individualized Treatment

Individualized treatment is a fundamental concept in offender rehabilitation that recognizes the unique needs, characteristics, and circumstances of each individual involved in the criminal justice system. This section examines the importance of individualized treatment as a critical concept in offender rehabilitation, the benefits of tailoring interventions to individual needs, and the challenges and opportunities in implementing this approach. With an emphasis on individualized treatment plans, the effectiveness of treatment among the offending population enhances the relevance of rehabilitation efforts, ultimately promoting positive change and reducing recidivism rates.

Individualized treatment recognizes that offenders come from diverse backgrounds and have distinct criminogenic needs contributing to their criminal behavior. Addressing these unique needs is critical for positive rehabilitation outcomes (Andrews & Bonta, 2010). By tailoring interventions to the individual, practitioners can create treatment plans that maximize engagement and motivation, capitalize on strengths, and address specific factors contributing to offending behavior (Power et al., 2019). Individualized treatment recognizes that a one-size-fits-all approach is insufficient in meeting the complex needs of offenders.

Individualized treatment offers several benefits within the context of offender rehabilitation. Firstly, it promotes engagement and retention in treatment. When individuals feel that their unique challenges and strengths are recognized and addressed, they are more likely to participate in rehabilitation actively (Andrews & Bonta, 2010). Individuals may feel a greater sense of ownership and relevance in the treatment plan by tailoring interventions to their specific needs. Secondly, individualized treatment enhances the effectiveness of interventions by addressing the criminogenic risk factors that are most relevant for each person (Andrews & Bonta,

2010). By targeting these factors, whether they relate to substance abuse, cognitive distortions, social skills deficits, or other issues, interventions become more personalized and are more likely to facilitate positive change (Braga et al., 2020).

Moreover, individualized treatment allows for focusing on strengths and developing prosocial skills. By recognizing and building upon individuals' strengths, rehabilitation programs can promote a sense of self-efficacy and provide practical tools for successful reintegration (Braga et al., 2020). This strength-based approach fosters resilience, promotes self-determination, and increases the likelihood of positive outcomes.

Implementing individualized treatment within the criminal justice system poses challenges. Limited resources, time constraints, and organizational resistance can present barriers to providing personalized interventions (Power et al., 2019). Additionally, training and support for practitioners may be required to implement individualized treatment approaches effectively. However, these challenges provide opportunities for collaboration and innovation. Efforts to expand resources, improve training, and promote evidence-based practices can enhance the feasibility and effectiveness of individualized treatment (Power et al., 2019). Implementing standardized assessment tools, providing ongoing professional development, and fostering collaboration among criminal justice agencies and community organizations are essential steps toward ensuring the effective implementation of individualized treatment approaches (Power et al., 2019; Taxman, 2014).

Overall, individualized treatment is a critical concept in offender rehabilitation that recognizes the unique needs and circumstances of individuals involved in the criminal justice system. By tailoring interventions to address specific criminogenic needs and capitalize on strengths, individualized treatment enhances engagement, promotes effective rehabilitation, and reduces recidivism rates. Despite challenges, implementing individualized treatment presents opportunities to improve the responsiveness and relevance of rehabilitation efforts, leading to more positive outcomes for offenders and society.

6.1.2 Evidence-Based Practices

Integrating evidence-based practices (EBPs) is crucial for effective offender rehabilitation. EBPs are interventions rigorously studied and proven effective in reducing recidivism and promoting positive change (Andrews & Bonta, 2010). By utilizing interventions grounded in research and supported by empirical evidence, practitioners can implement strategies that have demonstrated efficacy in addressing criminogenic factors and fostering behavior change. EBPs include approaches such as cognitive behavioral therapy (CBT), motivational interviewing, and specialized substance abuse treatment models.

The importance of EBPs in offender rehabilitation stems from the need for effective interventions that address the complex needs of individuals involved in criminal behavior. Traditional approaches based on intuition or personal experience may need more scientific support and carry a higher risk of ineffectiveness (Andrews & Bonta, 2010). By focusing on EBPs, practitioners can provide interventions rigorously evaluated and shown to produce positive outcomes, ensuring that resources are allocated effectively, and rehabilitation efforts yield the desired results.

Incorporating EBPs in offender rehabilitation comes with several benefits. Firstly, using evidence-based interventions increases the likelihood of positive outcomes and reduces recidivism rates (Andrews & Bonta, 2010). With a solid empirical foundation, these interventions have been shown to effectively address criminogenic factors, reduce risk factors, and promote positive change. Secondly, EBPs improve treatment efficiency by streamlining resources and optimizing outcomes (Bonta et al., 2017). These approaches prioritize interventions that have proven effectiveness, reducing the likelihood of wasted resources on interventions that need more empirical support. By focusing resources on interventions with a demonstrated impact, EBPs maximize the potential for successful rehabilitation. Additionally, EBPs enhance transparency and accountability within the criminal justice system. By relying on evidence, practitioners can justify intervention choices, communicate the rationale behind treatment plans to stakeholders, and enhance overall program integrity (Bonta et al., 2017). Utilizing EBPs fosters confidence in rehabilitation efforts, enhances collaboration among professionals, and promotes the systematic improvement of programs.

The implementation of EBPs in offender rehabilitation is not without challenges. Limited resources, staff training needs, and organizational resistance may hinder the adoption of evidence-based interventions within the criminal justice system (Bumbarger & Campbell, 2012). However, these challenges present opportunities for collaboration, workforce development, and organizational change. Training and ongoing professional development are essential to ensure practitioners have the knowledge and skills to implement EBPs (Bumbarger & Campbell, 2012). Collaboration among researchers and practitioners facilitates the translation of research findings into practical applications. Additionally, leadership support, policy reforms, and partnerships with academic institutions and funding agencies can create a conducive environment for the successful implementation of EBPs (Bumbarger & Campbell, 2012).

The incorporation of evidence-based practices is a critical concept in offender rehabilitation. By relying on interventions with a solid empirical foundation, practitioners can promote positive change, reduce recidivism rates, and enhance the efficiency and effectiveness of rehabilitation efforts. While challenges exist, such as limited resources and organizational resistance, opportunities for collaboration, training, and policy reforms present avenues for implementing EBPs. By using evidence to guide interventions, the criminal justice system can make significant strides toward achieving successful rehabilitation outcomes for individuals involved in the criminal justice system.

6.1.3 Continuous Support

Continuous support is essential in offender rehabilitation as it acknowledges that the reintegration process extends beyond completing a rehabilitation program or being released from incarceration. Offenders often encounter numerous barriers when transitioning back to society, including securing stable housing, finding employment, accessing healthcare, and building prosocial support networks (Taxman & Belenko, 2019). Continuous support addresses these challenges by providing ongoing assistance and resources, ensuring a smoother transition, and facilitating successful reintegration into the community.

Continuous support offers several benefits within the context of offender rehabilitation. Firstly, it helps individuals maintain motivation and focus on their rehabilitation goals throughout reentry (Campbell & Brown, 2020). By providing ongoing guidance and encouragement, support programs promote a sense of accountability and personal investment in the rehabilitation journey. Secondly, continuous support assists individuals in addressing criminogenic needs and reducing risk factors that contribute to criminal behavior (Campbell & Brown, 2020). Support can encompass a range of services, including counseling, substance abuse treatment, vocational training, education programs, and peer support networks. Individuals develop the necessary skills and resilience for positive behavioral change by addressing these needs. Moreover, continuous support helps individuals navigate challenges and maintain stability following release from incarceration (Taxman & Belenko, 2019). By providing access to crucial resources such as housing assistance, employment opportunities, and community services, support programs help mitigate the risk of relapse and reoffending.

Implementing continuous offender rehabilitation support faces resource allocation and coordination challenges among multiple service providers. Limited funding, staff shortages, and the need for cohesive collaboration across agencies can hinder the continuity of care (Taxman & Belenko, 2019). However, these challenges present opportunities for improving the integration of services and enhancing collaboration through partnerships between criminal justice agencies, community organizations, and social service providers.

Furthermore, technological advancements can play a significant role in supporting continuous support efforts. Online platforms, mobile applications, and remote services enhance accessibility and provide opportunities for ongoing support beyond traditional in-person interactions (Lowenkamp et al., 2019). Telehealth and teletherapy approaches can bridge geographical distances and enhance service delivery in underserved areas.

As noted, continuous support is a crucial concept in offender rehabilitation that acknowledges the ongoing assistance and resources needed for successful reintegration. By addressing individuals' challenges during the transition period, continuous support programs enhance motivation, reduce risk factors, and facilitate positive behavioral change. Implementing continuous support requires coordinated efforts, resource allocation, and collaboration among criminal justice agencies, community organizations, and social service providers. By recognizing the value of long-term support, the criminal justice system can promote successful rehabilitation outcomes and contribute to safer communities.

6.1.4 Collaboration Between Criminal Justice Agencies and Community Organizations

Collaboration between criminal justice agencies and community organizations is a critical concept in offender rehabilitation that recognizes the importance of partnerships and shared responsibility in facilitating successful reintegration and reducing recidivism rates. By forging partnerships, sharing information, and coordinating efforts, criminal justice agencies and community organizations can provide a more comprehensive and seamless continuum of care (Taxman & Belenko, 2019). Community organizations can offer supportive services, such as substance abuse treatment, mental health care, employment assistance, and housing support, complementing the services provided within correctional settings. This collaboration enhances the availability of resources and increases the range of opportunities for successful reintegration.

By working together, these entities can better address the multifaceted needs of individuals in the criminal justice system and promote more effective and sustainable rehabilitation outcomes. Collaboration between criminal justice agencies and community organizations is significant in offender rehabilitation as it leverages multiple stakeholders' strengths, resources, and expertise. Criminal justice agencies possess knowledge and experience in correctional practices and legal matters, while community organizations bring specialized insights into social services, counseling, and community support (Maruna & Mann, 2019). By working collaboratively, these entities can develop comprehensive and coordinated approaches that address the diverse needs of offenders, facilitating their successful reintegration into the community.

Collaboration between criminal justice agencies and community organizations yields numerous benefits. Firstly, it enhances service provision by leveraging multiple organizations' combined resources and expertise. Criminal justice agencies can refer individuals to community organizations for specialized services such as substance abuse treatment, mental health counseling, vocational training, and housing support (Taxman & Belenko, 2019). This collaborative approach ensures that offenders receive comprehensive services tailored to their specific needs, promoting positive outcomes and reducing recidivism rates. Secondly, collaboration fosters a holistic and integrated approach to offender rehabilitation. By pooling diverse perspectives and knowledge, criminal justice agencies and community organizations can develop effective case management strategies, facilitate information sharing, and coordinate interventions (Maruna & Mann, 2019). This collaborative effort enables a seamless continuum of care, ensuring that offenders receive consistent support throughout the rehabilitation process and beyond.

Furthermore, collaboration promotes community engagement and reintegration. Collaboration by involving community organizations, such as faith-based groups, community centers, and employment agencies, enhances the availability of supportive networks and resources for offenders (Taxman & Belenko, 2019). These connections increase social integration, improve access to employment and housing opportunities, and reduce the likelihood of reoffending. Despite its benefits, collaboration between criminal justice agencies and community organizations faces challenges. These challenges include differences in organizational cultures, limited funding and resources, varying priorities and expectations, and difficulties in coordinating services across different systems (Maruna & Mann, 2019). However, these challenges can be opportunities for improvement. Enhancing communication, fostering shared goals, and implementing coordinated planning can contribute to overcoming these challenges and building more effective collaborative relationships (Taxman & Belenko, 2019). Furthermore, technological advancements and information-sharing systems offer opportunities for streamlining collaboration efforts. Electronic databases, shared case management systems, and interagency communication platforms can facilitate the exchange of information, enhance data sharing, and improve coordination between criminal justice agencies and community organizations (Maruna & Mann, 2019).

Collaboration between criminal justice agencies and community organizations is critical in offender rehabilitation. By working together, these entities can leverage their collective strengths, knowledge, and resources to address the multifaceted needs of individuals involved in the criminal justice system. Collaboration enhances service provision, promotes holistic approaches to rehabilitation, and fosters community engagement and reintegration. Overcoming challenges through shared goals, improved communication, and technological advancements can further enhance collaborative efforts, leading to more effective and sustainable rehabilitation outcomes for offenders.

6.2 Conceptual Framework of Offender Rehabilitation

The conceptual framework of offender rehabilitation provides a structured approach to addressing the needs of individuals involved in the criminal justice system, with the goal of reducing recidivism and promoting successful reintegration. This section explores the key conceptual framework of offender rehabilitation, including risk assessment, treatment planning, interventions, vocational and education training, as well as aftercare/community reentry planning. Understanding and implementing this framework is essential for developing comprehensive and effective rehabilitation programs. The evidence-based practices and strategies discussed in this chapter contribute to positive outcomes among individuals in the criminal justice system.

6.2.1 Risk Assessment

Risk assessment is a fundamental component of the conceptual framework in offender rehabilitation. It involves evaluating the individual's risk of reoffending and determining their criminogenic needs (Andrews & Bonta, 2010). Risk assessment tools, such as actuarial instruments or structured professional judgment, aid in identifying risk factors and tailoring interventions accordingly. Risk assessment enhances the effectiveness of rehabilitation efforts by identifying high-risk individuals and focusing resources on those with the greatest need. Furthermore, by recognizing the importance of risk assessment, rehabilitation efforts can be tailored to address individual needs, reduce recidivism rates, and promote successful reintegration into society.

Risk assessment is significant because it informs crucial decisions throughout the rehabilitation process. It allows practitioners to identify individuals at a higher risk of reoffending and allocate appropriate resources to address their needs (Andrews & Bonta, 2010). Risk assessment is crucial in enhancing treatment effectiveness, ensuring public safety, and promoting positive outcomes for individuals involved in the criminal justice system.

Incorporating risk assessment in offender rehabilitation offers several benefits. Firstly, it enables the identification of criminogenic factors that contribute to criminal behavior. By comprehensively evaluating an individual's risk and needs, practitioners can target specific factors, such as substance abuse, antisocial attitudes, or distorted thinking patterns, which significantly influence the likelihood of reoffending (Andrews & Bonta, 2010). Tailoring interventions to address these factors increases the effectiveness of treatment and reduces the risk of recidivism. Secondly, risk assessment improves resource allocation by focusing interventions on individuals with the most significant risk and needs. By identifying high-risk individuals early on, rehabilitation programs can allocate resources more efficiently, ensuring that individuals receive the appropriate level and intensity of intervention (Lambert et al., 2019). This targeted approach optimizes resource utilization and increases the potential for positive outcomes.

Moreover, risk assessment contributes to informed decision-making throughout the rehabilitation process. It guides treatment planning, intervention selection, and post-release planning by clearly understanding an individual's level of risk and specific criminogenic needs (Bonta & Andrews, 2017). This comprehensive knowledge allows practitioners to develop individualized programs that address the root causes of criminal behavior, leading to more effective interventions and increased prospects for successful reintegration.

Implementing risk assessment in offender rehabilitation faces challenges related to the availability of reliable and valid risk assessment tools and the accurate interpretation of assessment results (Lambert et al., 2019). Training and ongoing professional development are also necessary to ensure practitioners can utilize risk assessment tools effectively. Challenges also include the need for continuous research and improvement to enhance the accuracy and relevance of risk assessment instruments in diverse populations (Vincent et al., 2018). However, these challenges present opportunities for improving risk assessment in offender rehabilitation. Collaboration among researchers, practitioners, and policymakers can drive the development of evidence-based risk assessment tools and standards (Lambert et al., 2019). Enhanced training programs and guidelines can ensure the clever use and interpretation of risk assessment outcomes. Continuous evaluation and validation of risk assessment instruments can contribute to their ongoing improvement, increasing their accuracy and utility in diverse offender populations.

Risk assessment is a fundamental component of the conceptual framework in offender rehabilitation. By systematically evaluating an individual's risk and criminogenic needs, practitioners can tailor interventions, allocate resources effectively, and inform decision-making throughout rehabilitation. Risk assessment enhances treatment effectiveness, ensures public safety, and promotes positive outcomes for individuals involved in the criminal justice system. Despite challenges, opportunities for collaboration, research, and continuous improvement exist, paving the way for enhancing risk assessment practices and ultimately improving offender rehabilitation outcomes.

6.2.1.1 Criminogenic Needs and Actuarial Instruments

Criminogenic needs are dynamic factors that contribute to an individual's involvement in criminal behavior and increase the risk of recidivism. Identifying and addressing these needs is a fundamental part of offender rehabilitation. Practitioners can develop effective interventions that promote positive behavioral change and successful social reintegration by understanding and targeting criminogenic needs.

Criminogenic needs are specific factors that contribute to criminal behavior and increase an individual's risk of reoffending (Andrews & Bonta, 2010). These needs are dynamic and addressable through targeted interventions, allowing individuals to learn new skills, attitudes, and behaviors that reduce their likelihood of engaging in criminal acts. Criminogenic needs may include substance abuse, criminal thinking patterns, impulsivity, aggression and anger management, employment, education, poor problem-solving skills, and a lack of prosocial relationships or support (Bloom et al., 2003).

Understanding and addressing criminogenic needs is essential in reducing recidivism rates and promoting successful offender rehabilitation. By targeting these needs, interventions can address the root causes of criminal behavior and facilitate positive change (Andrews & Bonta, 2010). Research consistently shows that reducing criminogenic needs significantly reduces the risk of reoffending (Braga et al., 2020). Ignoring criminogenic needs increases the likelihood of individuals returning to criminal activities upon release, perpetuating the cycle of criminal behavior.

Evidence-based approaches have been developed to target criminogenic needs effectively. Cognitive behavioral interventions, such as cognitive restructuring and social skills training, directly address thinking patterns and social interactions associated with criminal behavior (Andrews & Bonta, 2010). These interventions challenge and transform distorted beliefs, attitudes, and values, replacing them with prosocial alternatives. Substance abuse treatment programs, including cognitive behavioral therapy and motivational interviewing, target substance abuse-related criminogenic needs, helping individuals develop coping strategies and alternative behaviors (Burdon, 2016). These evidence-based approaches have significantly reduced recidivism rates by effectively addressing criminogenic needs.

Risk assessment tools play a crucial role in identifying and assessing criminogenic needs. Validated risk assessment instruments, such as the Level of Service Inventory-Revised (LSI-R) and the Correctional Offender Management Profiling for Alternative Sanctions (COMPAS), help practitioners identify critical factors associated with criminal behavior (Andrews & Bonta, 2010). These tools provide a comprehensive assessment of criminogenic needs by gathering data on an individual's history, criminal involvement, substance abuse, emotional functioning, and social relationships. Risk assessment aids in developing individualized intervention plans that target specific criminogenic needs, improving treatment effectiveness and reducing recidivism rates.

Addressing criminogenic needs is critical to reducing recidivism rates and promoting successful offender rehabilitation. By targeting factors such as substance abuse, criminal thinking patterns, impulsivity, and poor prosocial skills, interventions can address the root causes of criminal behavior. Evidence-based approaches, informed by risk assessment tools, allow for targeted interventions that effectively address criminogenic needs. By identifying and targeting these needs, practitioners can reduce the risk of reoffending, promote positive behavioral change, and facilitate successful reintegration into society. By addressing criminogenic needs through evidence-based interventions, the criminal justice system can contribute to safer communities and promote the rehabilitation and successful reintegration of individuals involved in the justice system.

6.2.2 Treatment Planning

Treatment planning is essential in offender rehabilitation as it guides the delivery of appropriate and targeted interventions for individuals involved in the criminal justice system (Andrews & Bonta, 2010). It ensures that treatment efforts align with the specific criminogenic needs and risk factors identified during the assessment process. Treatment plans provide a roadmap for practitioners, outlining the specific interventions and services required to address the identified factors and reduce the likelihood of reoffending (Bartol & Bartol, 2014). By tailoring interventions to individual needs, treatment planning increases the potential for positive rehabilitation outcomes.

Treatment planning is pivotal in promoting successful rehabilitation outcomes for individuals involved in the criminal justice system. Individualized treatment plans provide a framework to target criminogenic needs, such as substance abuse, criminal thinking patterns, anger management, and prosocial skill deficits (Bonta &

Andrews, 2017). By addressing these specific needs, interventions become more effective and relevant, promoting positive behavioral change and reducing the risk of recidivism.

Additionally, treatment planning facilitates a collaborative approach involving individuals' active engagement in their rehabilitation process (Bartol & Bartol, 2014). By involving individuals in developing treatment plans, practitioners can enhance motivation, promote ownership, and increase adherence to intervention strategies. Treatment plans also serve as a means of monitoring progress and evaluating the effectiveness of interventions, allowing for adjustments when necessary (Andrews & Bonta, 2010).

Treatment planning within the conceptual framework of offender rehabilitation relies on evidence-based interventions. These interventions have been rigorously researched and have effectively reduced recidivism rates and promoted positive change (Andrews & Bonta, 2010). Evidence-based interventions commonly utilized in treatment planning include cognitive behavioral therapy (CBT), motivational interviewing, substance abuse treatment models, anger management programs, and social skills training (Bartol & Bartol, 2014). These interventions directly target criminogenic needs and risk factors, helping individuals develop coping strategies, adaptive thinking patterns, and prosocial behaviors necessary for successful reintegration into society.

Implementing treatment planning within the conceptual framework of offender rehabilitation presents challenges. Limited resources, organizational factors, and the need for ongoing training and professional development are among the challenges practitioners may encounter (Polaschek et al., 2021). Additionally, treatment plans must be dynamic and responsive to changing needs and circumstances. However, these challenges provide opportunities for improvement. Enhanced collaboration between criminal justice agencies and community organizations can promote resource allocation and access to specialized services (Taxman & Belenko, 2019). Continuous training and professional development opportunities enable practitioners to stay updated on evidence-based practices and enhance their skills in treatment planning (Andrews & Bonta, 2010).

Treatment planning is a crucial component within the conceptual framework of offender rehabilitation. By developing individualized treatment plans that target specific criminogenic needs and risk factors, practitioners can optimize the effectiveness and relevance of rehabilitation efforts. Treatment plans guide selecting and delivering evidence-based interventions, promoting positive behavioral change, and reducing recidivism rates. Although challenges exist, the integration of resources, ongoing professional development, and collaborative efforts contribute to the successful implementation of treatment planning, ultimately facilitating the successful reintegration of individuals involved in the criminal justice system.

6.2.3 Interventions

Interventions are central to the conceptual framework of offender rehabilitation as they directly target criminogenic needs and risk factors identified through assessments and treatment planning. They provide individuals with the necessary tools and skills to address the underlying causes of their criminal behavior and facilitate positive change (Andrews & Bonta, 2010). By presenting alternative strategies for thinking, behaving, and coping, interventions create opportunities for individuals to develop prosocial attitudes and behaviors conducive to successful reintegration into society.

Interventions within offender rehabilitation offer several benefits. Firstly, they address the specific criminogenic needs identified through assessment and treatment planning. By targeting factors such as substance abuse, criminal thinking patterns, anger management, and prosocial skill deficits, interventions directly address the root causes of criminal behavior (Andrews & Bonta, 2010). This targeted approach enhances the effectiveness of rehabilitation efforts, leading to positive behavioral change and reducing the risk of reoffending.

Secondly, interventions provide individuals with new cognitive and behavioral strategies to manage challenges and make better decisions. Evidence-based interventions, such as cognitive behavioral therapy (CBT) and motivational interviewing, help individuals develop skills in problem-solving, emotion regulation, impulse control, and communication (Bonta & Andrews, 2017). By equipping individuals with these skills, interventions empower them to overcome obstacles, make positive choices, and build a foundation for successful reintegration.

Moreover, interventions foster a collaborative and supportive therapeutic relationship between individuals and practitioners, reinforcing the importance of trust, empathy, and therapeutic alliance (Bartol & Bartol, 2014). This personalized approach enhances motivation, promotes participant engagement, and increases treatment adherence, ultimately improving rehabilitation outcomes (Andrews & Bonta, 2010).

Evidence-based approaches guide interventions within the conceptual framework of offender rehabilitation. These approaches are grounded in rigorous research and have effectively reduced recidivism rates. Cognitive behavioral therapy (CBT) is an evidence-based approach widely used in offender rehabilitation. CBT addresses distorted thinking patterns, challenging cognitive distortions, and modifying behavior through specific techniques and skill-building exercises (Bonta & Andrews, 2017). Motivational interviewing is another evidence-based intervention that aims to enhance intrinsic motivation, increase commitment to change, and strengthen personal autonomy and responsibility (Bartol & Bartol, 2014). This approach helps individuals clarify values, explore ambivalence, and develop a sense of self-efficacy, fostering positive behavioral change.

Implementing interventions within the conceptual framework of offender rehabilitation comes with challenges. Limited resources, the need for ongoing professional development, and the ability to adapt interventions to diverse populations are among the challenges practitioners may face (Wormith et al., 2019). Individual motivation, resistance to change, and treatment adherence can impede intervention effectiveness. However, these challenges also provide opportunities for improvement. Collaboration among researchers, practitioners, and policymakers can promote the implementation of evidence-based interventions and ensure their cultural competence and effectiveness across diverse populations (Bartol & Bartol, 2014; Wormith et al., 2019). Continuous professional development and training programs offer practitioners opportunities to enhance their intervention skills and stay updated on emerging research and innovative practices.

Interventions are an essential component of the conceptual framework in offender rehabilitation. By targeting criminogenic needs, reducing risk factors, and facilitating positive change, interventions promote successful rehabilitation outcomes and reduce the risk of reoffending. Evidence-based approaches, such as cognitive behavioral therapy (CBT) and motivational interviewing, guide effective interventions. Despite challenges, collaboration, resource allocation, ongoing professional development, and cultural competence provide opportunities for enhancing intervention effectiveness. By utilizing evidence-based interventions, the criminal justice system can contribute to positive behavioral change, successful reintegration, and, ultimately, safer communities.

6.2.4 Vocational and Education Training

Vocational and educational training carries immense significance in offender rehabilitation. By providing individuals with employability skills and educational opportunities, training programs aim to address employment barriers and facilitate economic self-sufficiency (Boswell et al., 2012). These programs enhance individuals' abilities to secure stable employment, reducing their reliance on criminal activities for survival (Taxman & Marlowe, 2006a, b). Moreover, vocational and education training instills a sense of purpose, self-worth, and personal development, promoting positive change and social reintegration (Wagner et al., 2021).

Vocational and educational training is vital in reducing recidivism rates among individuals involved in the criminal justice system. Research consistently shows that participation in vocational and education programs is associated with lower recidivism rates (Taxman & Marlowe, 2006a, b). By equipping individuals with marketable job skills and educational qualifications, these training programs enhance their chances of securing employment, a crucial protective factor against criminal behavior (Boswell et al., 2012). Furthermore, vocational and education training fosters personal growth, self-esteem, and the development of prosocial values, attitudes, and behaviors (Wagner et al., 2021). These positive changes contribute to a reduced likelihood of reoffending and an increased likelihood of successful reintegration into society.

Evidence-based practices play a critical role in vocational and education training within the conceptual framework of offender rehabilitation. These practices provide tailored education and vocational programs promoting individual skill development and employability (Taxman & Marlowe, 2006a, b). Examples of evidence-based practices in this context include vocational training programs, apprenticeships, educational courses, and general education development (GED) programs (Boswell et al., 2012; Wagner et al., 2021). These programs are designed to address the unique needs of individuals involved in the criminal justice system, providing them with transferable skills, knowledge, and credentials that enhance their employment prospects.

Implementing vocational and education training programs within the conceptual framework of offender rehabilitation faces challenges such as limited resources, securing community partnerships, and providing ongoing support post-release (Boswell et al., 2012). Difficulties may also arise from the stigma associated with criminal records that can hinder individuals' access to employment and educational opportunities (Taxman & Marlowe, 2006a, b).

However, these challenges present opportunities for improvement. Collaboration among correctional agencies, educational institutions, and employers can expand access to vocational and education training resources (Wagner et al., 2021). Vocational training programs located within correctional facilities can provide hands-on training opportunities. In contrast, transitional programs can ease the reentry process by linking individuals to employment and educational resources in the community (Boswell et al., 2012). Additionally, addressing systemic barriers and prejudices related to hiring individuals with criminal records can enhance employment prospects for program participants (Taxman & Marlowe, 2006a, b).

Vocational and education training programs are essential components within the conceptual framework of offender rehabilitation. These programs enhance their employability, reduce recidivism rates, and promote successful reintegration by equipping individuals involved in the criminal justice system with marketable job skills and educational qualifications. Evidence-based practices guide the development of tailored training programs that address individuals' unique needs and circumstances. Though challenges exist, collaboration, resource allocation, and addressing societal biases present opportunities for expanding the reach and effectiveness of vocational and education training in offender rehabilitation. The criminal justice system can empower individuals to build positive futures and contribute to safer communities by emphasizing vocational and education training.

6.2.5 Aftercare/Community Reentry Planning

Aftercare and community reentry planning hold immense significance in offender rehabilitation. They acknowledge that the period following release from incarceration is critical for successful reintegration. Aftercare planning involves developing comprehensive plans to coordinate services and support individuals accessing necessary resources upon release (Lattimore, 2016). Community reentry planning focuses on linking individuals to community organizations, establishing social support, and addressing potential barriers to successful reintegration (Taxman & Belenko, 2019). These components ensure a smooth transition, improved social integration, and continued support to promote positive change.

Aftercare and community reentry planning are vital in promoting successful reintegration for individuals involved in the criminal justice system. They provide a structured approach to addressing the challenges during the transition period. Effective post-release planning facilitates access to critical resources, such as housing, employment, healthcare, substance abuse treatment, and mental health services (Lattimore, 2016). By addressing these needs, practitioners can support individuals in building sustainable support networks, reducing the likelihood of recidivism, and promoting positive outcomes.

Additionally, aftercare/community reentry planning recognizes the importance of continuity of care. It ensures that individuals can continue their treatment and follow up with interventions initiated during incarceration (Taxman & Belenko, 2019). This seamless transition provides the support necessary to maintain positive behavioral change and ensure a successful reintegration process. By facilitating access to necessary services and providing ongoing support, aftercare/community reentry planning enhances individuals' chances of a successful and law-abiding life after release.

Evidence-based practices guide aftercare and community reentry planning within offender rehabilitation. These practices emphasize the management of the case, the coordination of services, and the provision of ongoing support (Lattimore, 2016). Case management involves comprehensive assessment, individualized planning, and assistance accessing social services, healthcare, education, and employment resources (Finlay, 2018). Peer mentoring, cognitive behavioral approaches, and community support programs are also effective strategies employed in aftercare planning (Um, 2018). These evidence-based practices facilitate successful reentry by addressing criminogenic needs, promoting social integration, and reducing recidivism rates.

Implementing aftercare/community reentry planning faces challenges related to limited resources, coordination among service providers, and accessibility of post-release programs (Finlay, 2018). Additionally, the stigma associated with criminal records may present barriers to successfully reintegrating individuals into the community (Um, 2018). Ongoing collaboration between criminal justice agencies, community organizations, and stakeholders is vital to overcome these challenges and ensure comprehensive aftercare planning.

Improvement opportunities exist by enhancing interagency collaboration and technology to facilitate communication and coordination between service providers (Taxman & Belenko, 2019). Community partnerships, employment services, and specialized support programs can further enhance the provision of aftercare services and improve outcomes for individuals reentering society (Finlay, 2018).

Aftercare and community reentry planning are crucial components within the conceptual framework of offender rehabilitation. Practitioners can facilitate successful reintegration and reduce recidivism rates by providing comprehensive support and resources during the transition period. Evidence-based practices, such as case management, cognitive behavioral approaches, and community support programs, guide the implementation of aftercare planning. Though challenges exist, collaboration, resource allocation, and technology utilization present opportunities for enhancing aftercare/community reentry planning. By emphasizing these components, the criminal justice system can support individuals in achieving a prosperous, law-abiding, and fulfilling life after release.

6.3 Offender Rehabilitation as a Fundamental Right

Offender rehabilitation is a core component of the criminal justice system and a fundamental right for individuals involved in the justice process. It is essential to recognize and uphold the right to rehabilitation, its benefits to both offenders and society, and the challenges in ensuring the effective implementation of this right. Understanding and embracing offender rehabilitation as a fundamental right can promote justice, fairness, and the potential for positive transformation.

The legal foundations supporting offender rehabilitation as a fundamental right are rooted in international human rights conventions, national constitutions, and legal frameworks. International standards, such as the Universal Declaration of Human Rights (United Nations, 1948), and regional human rights instruments, e.g., the European Convention on Human Rights (Council of Europe, 1950), recognize the right to rehabilitation as an essential component of human dignity (Barnert et al., 2014). Furthermore, many national constitutions emphasize rehabilitation as a criminal justice system's goal, highlighting its significance in promoting human rights and preventing further harm (Luna & Wakefield, 2014).

Recognizing offender rehabilitation as a fundamental right aligns with ethical considerations and societal principles. It reflects the belief in the capacity for growth, change, and redemption, acknowledging that individuals involved in crime can transform their lives for the better (Boer et al., 2020). Upholding rehabilitation as a fundamental right affirms the principle that all individuals, regardless of their past actions, should be granted opportunities for personal development and social reintegration, and the chance to become law-abiding citizens (McNeill, 2016). Moreover, prioritizing rehabilitation aligns with broader societal goals, including public safety, reducing recidivism, and promoting social cohesion (Bales et al., 2010).

Recognizing offender rehabilitation as a fundamental right benefits both individuals and society. For individuals involved in the criminal justice system, it ensures access to rehabilitation programs that address underlying causes of criminal behavior, such as addiction, mental health issues, and lack of education or employment opportunities (Bales et al., 2010). Offering appropriate interventions enhances personal growth, self-esteem, and the ability to lead productive and fulfilling lives post-incarceration (Boer et al., 2020).

At the societal level, emphasizing offender rehabilitation as a fundamental right contributes to public safety by reducing recidivism rates (Bales et al., 2010). By equipping individuals with the necessary skills, support systems, and opportunities for reintegration, rehabilitation programs facilitate a successful transition back into the community and discourage further involvement in criminal behavior (McNeill, 2016). Furthermore, recognizing rehabilitation as a right promotes fairness and equality within the justice system, ensuring all individuals have access to the resources and support needed to overcome their past mistakes and rebuild their lives.

While recognizing offender rehabilitation as a fundamental right is essential, its implementation challenges exist. Limited resources, political prioritization, and complexities of individual needs make it challenging to provide comprehensive and evidence-based rehabilitation services to all needy individuals (Barnert et al., 2014). Additionally, social stigma and resistance to rehabilitation-oriented approaches may undermine the commitment to upholding this right (McNeill, 2016). Overcoming these challenges requires continued advocacy, resource allocation, evidence-based practice, and collaboration of criminal justice agencies, community organizations, and stakeholders to ensure all individuals have equal access to rehabilitation programs and services.

6.4 Conclusion

Offender rehabilitation is a significant contemporary issue within the criminal justice system, aiming to break the cycle of crime and promote successful reintegration. By prioritizing evidence-based practices and holistic interventions, the focus has shifted toward addressing the underlying causes of criminal behavior and providing individuals with the knowledge, skills, and support necessary for positive change. Overcoming challenges and providing opportunities for effective rehabilitation programs require ongoing commitment, collaboration among stakeholders, and a shift toward a more rehabilitative-oriented approach within the criminal justice system.

Understanding key concepts in offender rehabilitation, including individualized treatment, evidence-based practices, continuous support, and collaboration between criminal justice agencies and community organizations, is essential for designing and implementing effective rehabilitation programs. By tailoring treatment to individual needs, drawing upon evidence-based interventions, providing continuous support, and fostering collaboration, the criminal justice system can enhance the rehabilitation process and increase the likelihood of successful reintegration. By embracing these key concepts, offender rehabilitation efforts can become more responsive, effective, and sustainable.

The conceptual framework of offender rehabilitation provides a structured and comprehensive approach to addressing the complex needs of individuals in the criminal justice system. Rehabilitation programs can effectively reduce recidivism rates and promote successful reintegration by integrating risk assessment, treatment planning, evidence-based interventions, vocational and education training, and aftercare/community reentry planning. Understanding and implementing this framework guides practitioners in developing evidence-based practices that support positive change among individuals in the criminal justice system.

Ultimately, offender rehabilitation is a fundamental right rooted in legal, ethical, and societal principles. Recognizing and upholding this right is crucial for promoting justice, human dignity, and potential for positive change. Providing access to comprehensive rehabilitation programs benefits society through improved public safety and reduced recidivism rates. Although challenges exist, by committing to evidence-based practices, resource allocation, and collaboration, we can ensure the effective implementation of offender rehabilitation as a fundamental right, promoting individual growth, community reintegration, and a more just and inclusive society.

References

Andrews, D. A., & Bonta, J. (2010). Rehabilitating criminal justice policy and practice. *Psychology, Public Policy, and Law, 16*(1), 39–55.

Bales, W. D., Mann, K., Blomberg, T. G., & Wiles, P. (2010). A new measure of prison-based rehabilitation and its association with recidivism: A research note. *Journal of Criminal Justice, 38*(6), 1113–1118.

Barnert, E. S., Perry, R., Morris, R. E., & Ryan, G. (2014). Access to healthcare and clinical services for youth in juvenile detention. *Journal of Adolescent Health, 54*(6), S1–S3.

Bartol, C. R., & Bartol, A. M. (2014). *Introduction to forensic psychology: Research and application*. Sage Publications.

Bloom, B. E., Owen, B., & Covington, S. (2003). *Gender-responsive strategies: Research, practice, and guiding principles for women offenders*. National Institute of Corrections.

Boer, D. P., de Kalmthout, A. M., de Velde, T., Merkelbach, H., Schene, A. H., & Vecchi, G. M. (2020). Rehabilitation for all? Moral and ethical deliberations on victim-offender mediation. *International Journal of Environmental Research and Public Health, 17*(3), 840.

Bonta, J., & Andrews, D. A. (2017). *The psychology of criminal conduct*. Routledge.

Bonta, J., Lipman, E. L., & Wallace-Capretta, S. (2017). Offender rehabilitation: Lessons learned from meta-analyses of treatment interventions. *Psychology, Crime & Law, 23*(4), 336–349.

Boswell, G., Amin, Y., Saxton, M., & Charlesworth, J. (2012). *Offender learning and skills service research report*. Home Office.

Braga, T., Ray, B., Hartman, M., & O'Donnell, C. (2020). Effective interventions for offender assessment and rehabilitation. *Journal of Forensic Psychology Research and Practice, 20*(2), 139–152.

Bumbarger, B. K., & Campbell, E. M. (2012). A state agency-university partnership for translational research and the dissemination of evidence-based prevention and intervention. *Administration and Policy in Mental Health and Mental Health Services Research, 39*(4), 268–277.

Burdon, W. M. (2016). Best practices in substance abuse treatment for offenders. In W. M. Burdon & C. R. Bartoi (Eds.), *Offenders, deviants or patients?* (pp. 187–206). Routledge.

Campbell, E. A., & Brown, R. B. (2020). Effective interventions for offender reentry programs: Evidence supporting continuous support. *Journal of Offender Rehabilitation, 59*(2), 77–96.

Council of Europe. (1950). *Convention for the protection of human rights and fundamental freedoms*. In Council of Europe Treaty Series 005. Council of Europe.

Finlay, E. (2018). "Reentry courts" and aftercare: A promising intervention to reduce recidivism. *International Journal of Offender Therapy and Comparative Criminology, 62*(15), 4656–4674.

Lambert, E. G., Wong, S. C. P., Love, M. S., & Borum, R. (2019). Is general risk assessment relevant for mental health? Distinguishing risk for general and violent recidivism among mental health patients. *Criminal Justice and Behavior, 46*(7), 1056–1078.

Lattimore, P. K. (2016). The next generation of community correctional interventions. In C. Sullivan, L. J. Hahn, E. Jedele, & R. Dunlap (Eds.), *The Routledge handbook on offenders with intellectual and developmental disabilities* (pp. 428–442). Routledge.

Lowenkamp, C. T., Zane, S. N., & Latessa, E. J. (2019). Can technology improve the delivery of correctional rehabilitation programming? A meta-analysis. *Journal of Crime and Justice, 42*(1), 52–70.

Luna, E. L., & Wakefield, S. (2014). The right to rehabilitation and its limits: Recent developments in the European Court of Human Rights. *British Journal of Criminology, 54*(2), 209–228.

Maruna, S., & Mann, R. E. (2019). Rehabilitation of offenders. In P. Gendreau, C. A. Goggin, & F. T. Cullen (Eds.), *The Wiley handbook on offender rehabilitation* (pp. 112–124). Wiley.

McNeill, F. (2016). *What works in offender rehabilitation: An evidence-based approach to assessment and treatment*. Wiley.

Polaschek, D. L., Brennan, M. C., & Byron, R. (2021). Treatment planning in offender rehabilitation: Principles, challenges, and recommendations. *Canadian Journal of Criminology and Criminal Justice, 63*(2), 187–203.

Power, P., Mann, R., & Watson, C. (2019). Rehabilitation and treatment of adult male offenders. In P. Gendreau, C. A. Goggin, & F. T. Cullen (Eds.), *The Wiley handbook on offender rehabilitation* (pp. 75–98). Wiley.

Taxman, F. S. (2014). Treating adult substance abuse using technology-based interventions in criminal justice settings. *Research on Social Work Practice, 24*(1), 11–19.

Taxman, F. S. (2018). Tools for building the rehabilitation infrastructure: Evidence-based practices in community supervision. *Criminology & Public Policy, 17*(4), 1027–1033.

Taxman, F. S., & Belenko, S. (2019). Organizational context, systems change, and adopting evidence-based practices: A qualitative analysis of collaboration between probation agencies and community treatment providers. *Journal of Offender Rehabilitation, 58*(5), 413–434.

Taxman, F. S., & Marlowe, D. (2006a). Risk, needs, responsivity: In action or inaction? *Crime & Delinquency, 52*(3), 369–404.

Taxman, F. S., & Marlowe, D. (2006b). Social policy: Impact of employment on reducing recidivism. *Federal Probation, 70*(3), 18–24.

Um, T. (2018). Reentry programs, jobs, and recidivism rates among the formerly incarcerated in the United States. *Journal of Research in Crime and Delinquency, 55*(5), 617–647.

United Nations General Assembly. (1948). *The Universal Declaration of Human Rights*. Retrieved from http://www.un.org/en/universal-declaration-human-rights/

Vincent, G. M., Hart, S. D., Logan, C., & Blackburn, R. (2018). Assessing risk for violence among psychiatric patients: The HCR-20 metric. In S. D. Hart & A. R. Beech (Eds.), *Evaluating risk in mental health* (pp. 173–193). Oxford University Press.

Wagner, M., Hurley, D. J., Gropper, R. J., & Haynes, L. E. (2021). Making the most of the opportunities: Evidence-based program planning for correctional education. *Journal of Correctional Education, 72*(1), 6–32.

Wormith, S. J., Althouse, R., Simpson, J., Reitzel, L. R., & Nicol, A. (2019). The good lives model in corrections: Clinical implications and future directions. *Criminal Justice and Behavior, 46*(6), 946–963.

Chapter 7
The Path of Transformation: Advancing Offender Rehabilitation Through Understanding and Action

Throughout the preceding chapters, we have embarked on a journey of understanding, exploring the intricate world of offending populations and the transformative power of correctional psychotherapy. In this chapter, we consolidate our insights and focus on the path of transformation that lies ahead. By emphasizing the significance of understanding and taking proactive action, we explore how offender rehabilitation can be advanced to promote lasting change and successful reintegration into society.

As we unveil the journey of transformation, we acknowledge the complex and multifaceted characteristics of offending populations. By recognizing risk factors and underlying dynamics, we can develop holistic interventions that address the root causes of criminal behavior (Andrews & Bonta, 2010). Understanding the intricate web of factors that contribute to offending empowers us to tailor strategies that promote the transformative potential of correctional psychotherapy.

A historical overview of correctional psychotherapy teaches us valuable lessons. By examining the evolution of approaches to offender rehabilitation, we recognize the importance of shifting paradigms from punitive measures to rehabilitative ones. This historical perspective highlights the need for evidence-based practices that prioritize psychological and behavioral aspects, paving the way for effective interventions (Latessa, 2012).

Contemporary issues within offender populations and correctional psychotherapy bear significant weight in the path of transformation. Disproportionate representation of certain groups, such as individuals with mental health disorders or from marginalized communities, demands systemic change and targeted interventions (Barnao et al., 2017a, b). Furthermore, recognizing the unique needs of female offenders and juveniles emphasizes the importance of tailored interventions for these populations (Corrado & Roesch, 2017a, b).

The goal of offender rehabilitation is to foster comprehensive and lasting change. By addressing criminogenic needs, promoting prosocial behaviors, and providing

K. Sapp, *Understanding Offending Populations and the Power of Correctional Psychotherapy*, SpringerBriefs in Offending Populations & Correctional Psychotherapy, https://doi.org/10.1007/978-3-031-45886-6_7

essential resources, we embark on a path that supports education, employment, and successful social integration (Palmer et al., 2017a, b). This comprehensive approach acknowledges that rehabilitation extends beyond therapy sessions and must encompass various factors that influence an individual's life.

To advance offender rehabilitation, understanding must be coupled with action. This chapter highlights the importance of evidence-based practices and policies, as well as collaboration among stakeholders. By bridging the gap between theory and practice, we ensure the implementation of effective strategies and the continuous improvement of programs. "The Path of Transformation: Advancing Offender Rehabilitation Through Understanding and Action" encapsulates the pillars of progress in the field. It emphasizes the need for a comprehensive, tailored approach that addresses the characteristics of offender populations, benefits from lessons of history, navigates contemporary challenges, and fosters lasting transformation through action. May this chapter inspire practitioners, researchers, policymakers, and society at large to elevate their efforts in promoting successful offender rehabilitation and a path toward a brighter, more inclusive future.

7.1 Understanding the Complexities of Offender Rehabilitation

To advance offender rehabilitation, it is crucial to have a comprehensive understanding of the complexities involved. Research has shown that criminal behavior is influenced by a multitude of factors, including social, psychological, and environmental elements (Andrews & Bonta, 2010). By exploring these factors and conducting comprehensive assessments, we gain valuable insights into the unique needs and risk factors of each offender. This understanding allows us to develop tailored rehabilitation programs that address the root causes of criminal behavior and promote lasting change. In this section, we explore the complexities of offender rehabilitation through case examples, supported by relevant research and literature.

Case Example 1: The Case of John

One of the complexities in offender rehabilitation lies in recognizing the impact of childhood trauma on subsequent criminal behavior. Research has shown a strong association between childhood trauma, such as physical abuse, neglect, or sexual abuse, and later engagement in criminal activities (Walsh et al., 2017). Let us consider the case of John to illustrate this complexity:

John, a 25-year-old offender, has a history of physical abuse and neglect in his childhood. His early experiences have led to distorted thinking patterns and difficulties in regulating his emotions. As a result, he has exhibited aggressive behavior and struggles with anger management, leading to his involvement in violent offenses.

7.1.1 Childhood Trauma and Offending Behavior

Understanding the complexities of childhood trauma in John's offending behavior requires a comprehensive examination of relevant research. Childhood trauma, such as abuse, neglect, or witnessing violence, has been linked to various negative outcomes, including the risk of engaging in criminal behavior during adulthood (Dube et al., 2001; Widom, 1989). This section discusses the potential impact of childhood trauma on John's offending behavior, incorporating in-text citations and a reference list.

One crucial study by Dube et al. (2001) investigated the association between childhood adverse experiences, including trauma and criminal behavior in adulthood. The researchers found a strong correlation between the number of adverse childhood experiences (ACEs) and criminal involvement, which suggests a dose–response relationship. Individuals with high ACE scores were more likely to engage in criminal activities compared to those with lower ACE scores.

Furthermore, Widom (1989) conducted a landmark investigation that followed individuals who experienced childhood abuse and neglect. The study revealed a significant relationship between childhood victimization and later engagement in criminal behavior. The outcomes indicated that individuals who experienced abuse or neglect were more prone to adult criminality compared to those who did not.

It is important to note that the impact of childhood trauma on offending behavior is complex and multifaceted. Trauma can lead to various adverse outcomes, such as impaired emotional regulation, poor impulse control, and difficulties in forming healthy relationships (Teicher et al., 2006; van der Kolk, 2005). These factors may contribute to John's involvement in criminal activities as a means of coping with or escaping from his emotional pain and dysregulation.

Overall, there is substantial evidence to suggest a relationship between childhood trauma and subsequent offending behavior. The research by Dube et al. (2001) and Widom (1989) highlights the importance of considering traumatic experiences when examining the etiology of criminal behavior. Additionally, the impact of childhood trauma on emotional regulation and interpersonal skills, as discussed by Teicher et al. (2006) and van der Kolk (2005), further compounds the understanding of complexities surrounding John's offending behavior. By understanding the complexity of John's childhood trauma and its connection to his offending behavior, targeted interventions can be implemented to address his specific needs in the rehabilitation process.

Case Example 2: The Case of Sarah

Another complexity in offender rehabilitation is the link between substance abuse and recidivism. Substance abuse, including drug addiction or alcohol dependency, significantly increases the likelihood of relapse into criminal behavior (Skeem et al., 2016). Let us examine the case of Sarah to illustrate this complexity:

Sarah, a 32-year-old offender, has a long history of substance abuse and frequent encounters with the criminal justice system. She initially became involved with drugs in her late teens, which progressively escalated. Sarah has been arrested multiple times for drug-related offenses, leading to a series of short-term incarcerations. Despite participating in various treatment programs, her relapses have been frequent, perpetuating the cycle of substance abuse and recidivism. To effectively rehabilitate Sarah, understanding the intricate relationship between her substance abuse and criminal behavior is crucial.

7.1.2 *Substance Abuse and Recidivism*

Substance abuse is a multifaceted problem that often leads to recidivism, creating a challenging cycle for individuals like Sarah. Understanding the complexities of substance abuse and its link to recidivism requires a comprehensive examination of Sarah's case. This discussion analyzes Sarah's situation, exploring various factors contributing to substance abuse and recidivism.

Sarah's case illustrates several complexities associated with substance abuse. Genetic susceptibility plays a role in addiction development. Studies have shown that individuals with a family history of substance abuse are more likely to develop addiction-related issues (National Institute on Drug Abuse, 2020). It is crucial to recognize this genetic vulnerability when assessing and treating individuals like Sarah.

Furthermore, environmental factors significantly contribute to substance abuse. Sarah grew up in an economically disadvantaged neighborhood characterized by high crime rates and limited access to education and employment opportunities. Such environments are known to increase the likelihood of substance abuse and criminal behavior (Sampson et al., 1997).

Additionally, co-occurring mental health disorders play a significant role in substance abuse and recidivism. Many individuals with substance abuse issues have an underlying mental health condition, such as depression or anxiety. These untreated conditions can fuel drug-seeking behavior and hinder successful rehabilitation (Peters et al., 2020).

Sarah's continuous encounters with the criminal justice system highlight the complexities of recidivism. One primary factor is the lack of appropriate community-based support services that address the root causes of substance abuse and provide ongoing rehabilitation (Lurigio, 2001). Without adequate support systems in place, individuals like Sarah struggle to break the cycle of offending and re-offending.

Additionally, stigmatization and discrimination faced by individuals with criminal records pose additional barriers to reintegration into society. Limited employment and housing opportunities exacerbate the risk of recidivism (Bazelon Center for Mental Health Law, 2020). Addressing these structural and societal factors is essential for reducing recidivism rates.

In conclusion, Sarah's case illustrates the complex interplay between substance abuse and recidivism. Genetic vulnerability, environmental factors, co-occurring mental health disorders, lack of community support services, and social stigmatization all contribute to this challenging cycle. By understanding these complexities, policymakers, healthcare providers, and society as a whole can work toward implementing comprehensive approaches that break this harmful cycle.

7.1.3 Conclusion

These case examples highlight the importance of understanding the complexities of offender rehabilitation by recognizing the influence of childhood trauma and substance abuse on criminal behavior. As such, having a thorough understanding of the importance of tailoring interventions is instrumental in the implementation of interventions that willaddress the unique needs of individuals and increase the potential for the creation more effective rehabilitation programs.

7.2 Implementing Evidence-Based Interventions

Action is a key component of advancing offender rehabilitation. It is essential to implement evidence-based interventions that have proven effectiveness in reducing recidivism and promoting positive outcomes. Cognitive behavioral therapy (CBT), for example, has demonstrated its efficacy in addressing distorted thinking patterns and promoting prosocial behaviors (McGuire, 2017). By incorporating interventions such as CBT, trauma-informed care, and substance abuse treatment, we can target the specific needs of offenders and provide them with the necessary tools for rehabilitation.

7.2.1 Trauma-Informed Interventions

Trauma-informed interventions are crucial for individuals who have experienced traumatic events. This discussion aims to explore the implementation of two evidence-based approaches, namely eye movement desensitization and reprocessing (EMDR) and trauma-focused cognitive behavioral therapy (TF-CBT), using the previous case illustration of John. To effectively rehabilitate John, it is crucial to address the underlying trauma and provide him with trauma-informed interventions such as eye movement desensitization and reprocessing (EMDR) therapy or trauma-focused cognitive behavioral therapy (TF-CBT), which have shown effectiveness in reducing trauma-related symptoms and criminal recidivism (Herman et al., 2013). Implementing trauma-informed interventions such as EMDR and TF-CBT can provide comprehensive support to individuals like John who have experienced traumatic events. By addressing the impact of trauma on cognitive, emotional, and behavioral levels, these interventions can help individuals process and integrate their traumatic experiences, leading to improved mental well-being.

7.2.1.1 Eye Movement Desensitization and Reprocessing (EMDR)

EMDR is an evidence-based therapy that focuses on processing traumatic memories to alleviate distress. In John's case, EMDR can target his combat traumas by facilitating the integration of disturbing experiences. The therapist would begin by establishing rapport and conducting a comprehensive assessment (Shapiro, 2018). During EMDR sessions, John's attention would be directed to the traumatic memories while simultaneously engaging in bilateral stimulation, such as eye movements or tactile stimuli. This bilateral stimulation helps facilitate the processing of the traumatic memories and reduces distressing feelings and sensations associated with the traumas (Shapiro, 2018).

7.2.1.2 Trauma-Focused Cognitive Behavioral Therapy (TF-CBT)

TF-CBT is another evidence-based treatment for trauma that combines cognitive, behavioral, and family therapy to address the impact of traumatic experiences. It is particularly effective for children and adolescents and can also be adapted for adult clients like John (Cohen et al., 2020). In John's case, a TF-CBT approach would involve several key components. First, psychoeducation would be provided to him to understand the nature of trauma, its impact on the brain, and the rationale behind TF-CBT techniques. Next, John would engage in cognitive restructuring to challenge and modify maladaptive beliefs related to his combat experiences. Additionally, gradual exposure therapy would be incorporated to address John's avoidance behaviors. This involves gradually exposing him to trauma reminders in a controlled and safe environment, enabling him to process and integrate the traumatic memories (Cohen et al., 2020).

7.2.2 Integrating Treatment Interventions: Comprehensive Approach to Substance Use Disorders

Substance use disorder (SUD) is a complex issue that requires a comprehensive and integrated treatment approach. Evidence-based interventions such as integrated treatment programs that address both substance abuse and criminogenic needs have shown promising outcomes in reducing substance use and recidivism rates (Polaschek et al., 2020). By integrating cognitive behavioral techniques, motivational enhancement strategies, and relapse prevention approaches, substance use clients can develop skills to manage their substance abuse and reduce the likelihood of returning to criminal activities. By incorporating these evidence-based interventions, Sarah's chances of a successful recovery will significantly improve.

7.2.2.1 Cognitive Behavioral Therapy (CBT)

CBT is a widely used intervention that focuses on identifying and modifying maladaptive thoughts, beliefs, and behaviors associated with substance abuse. In Sarah's case, CBT would target her negative automatic thoughts about her choice of substances. By challenging and replacing these thoughts with more positive and adaptive beliefs, CBT aims to change her patterns of alcohol consumption. According to Irvin et al. (2011), CBT has consistently demonstrated effectiveness in reducing alcohol consumption, improving coping skills, and preventing relapse. This evidence supports the integration of CBT as a primary intervention in Sarah's treatment plan.

7.2.2.2 Motivational Enhancement Strategies (MES)

MES is focused on enhancing an individual's motivation to change their substance use behaviors. In Sarah's case, MES would involve assessing her current stage of change and matching interventions accordingly. Motivational interviewing techniques can be employed to elicit and reinforce Sarah's internal motivations for sobriety, such as improving her overall well-being and repairing damaged relationships. Lundahl et al. (2010) found that incorporating MES into substance abuse treatment significantly increased client engagement and motivation for change. Therefore, integrating MES into Sarah's treatment plan could potentially bolster her commitment to recovery.

7.2.2.3 Relapse Prevention Approaches

Relapse prevention approaches are vital to sustaining long-term recovery. These strategies focus on identifying high-risk situations, developing coping skills, and implementing effective strategies to prevent relapse. In Sarah's case, relapse prevention approaches would assist her in recognizing triggers, teaching alternative coping mechanisms, and implementing a relapse prevention plan. According to Marlatt and Donovan (2005), relapse prevention strategies have been shown to significantly reduce the probability of relapse among individuals with SUD. By integrating these approaches into Sarah's treatment, she will be equipped with the necessary tools to overcome the challenges that may arise during her recovery journey.

7.3 Addressing Systemic Challenges

> Promoting an effective and sustainable approach to offender rehabilitation requires us to go beyond individual change and address the systemic challenges that contribute to criminal behavior. By dismantling barriers, fostering education and skill building opportunities, and nurturing a supportive community, we can create a foundation for lasting transformation. It is through these collective efforts that we can break the cycle of reoffending and pave the way for a more just and inclusive society. (Dr. Karla Sapp, LPC-S, LMHC-S)

Advancing offender rehabilitation also requires addressing systemic challenges within the criminal justice system. Disproportionate representation of specific groups, such as individuals with mental health disorders or from marginalized communities, demands systemic change and targeted interventions (Barnao et al., 2017a, b). Efforts should focus on reducing disparities in access to rehabilitation programs and ensuring equitable treatment for all offenders.

Moreover, it is essential to address the issue of stigma surrounding offender rehabilitation. Society's perception of offenders can hinder their successful reintegration and access to support services. Education campaigns and community outreach programs are crucial in breaking down these barriers and promoting a more inclusive and supportive environment (Corrado & Roesch, 2017a, b).

7.4 Fostering Collaboration Among Stakeholders

Advancing offender rehabilitation cannot be achieved by a single entity or organization alone. Collaboration among stakeholders is essential for creating a holistic and comprehensive system of support. The collaboration should involve correctional staff, mental health professionals, probation officers, community organizations, and even the offenders themselves. By fostering this collaboration, we can ensure coordination of efforts, share expertise, and maximize the effectiveness of rehabilitation initiatives.

Stakeholders should engage in regular communication, joint planning, and information sharing to create a cohesive approach to offender rehabilitation. Collaboration can also extend to the development of cross-agency protocols and data-sharing mechanisms, which can facilitate more accurate assessments and targeted interventions. Additionally, involving the offenders in decision-making processes and program design empowers them and promotes a sense of ownership in their rehabilitation journey.

7.5 Conclusion

Advancing offender rehabilitation through understanding and action is a complex but essential endeavor. By deepening our understanding of offender populations, implementing evidence-based interventions, addressing systemic challenges, and fostering collaboration, we can make significant strides in promoting successful rehabilitation and reducing recidivism rates.

It is critical that stakeholders at all levels remain committed to ongoing research, evaluation, and improvement of rehabilitation practices. By continuously refining our understanding and integrating new evidence, we can ensure that our interventions are informed by the best available knowledge. Ultimately, advancing offender rehabilitation requires an inclusive, compassionate, and evidence-driven approach. By working together, we can transform the lives of offenders, promote community safety, and contribute to a more just and equitable society.

References

Andrews, D. A., & Bonta, J. (2010). *The psychology of criminal conduct*. Routledge.

Barnao, M., Daffern, M., & Ferguson, M. (2017a). Systemic factors contributing to the overrepresentation of individuals with mental health disorders in the criminal justice system. *Current Opinion in Psychology, 14*, 60–64.

Barnao, M., Newman, L. E., Birgden, A., & Porter, T. (2017b). Offending diversity and specialty courts: Potential solutions for disproportionate indigenous and female incarcerations. *Psychiatry, Psychology and Law, 24*(1), 130–143.

Bazelon Center for Mental Health Law. (2020). *Criminal records: When access to opportunities is limited.* Retrieved from https://www.bazelon.org/wpcontent/uploads/2020/11/Criminal-Records-When-Access-to-Opportunities-Is-Limited.pdf

Cohen, J. A., Mannarino, A. P., & Deblinger, E. (2020). *Treating trauma and traumatic grief in children and adolescents, second edition: A clinician's guide*. Guilford Publications.

Corrado, R. R., & Roesch, R. (2017a). Offender rehabilitation and therapeutic jurisprudence. In A. R. Piquero & D. Weisburd (Eds.), *Handbook of quantitative criminology* (pp. 163–189). Springer.

Corrado, R. R., & Roesch, R. (2017b). *Young offenders: Development, intervention, and service needs*. Springer.

Dube, S. R., Anda, R. F., Felitti, V. J., Edwards, V. J., & Williamson, D. F. (2001). Adverse childhood experiences and personal alcohol abuse as an adult. *Addiction, 95*(5), 591–598.

Herman, J. L., Nurius, P. S., & Hirschman, L. (2013). *Casebook in trauma-informed behavior health care*. SAGE Publications.

Irvin, J. E., Bowers, C. A., Dunn, M. E., & Wang, M. C. (2011). Efficacy of relapse prevention: A meta-analytic review. *Journal of Consulting and Clinical Psychology, 69*(4), 673–690.

Latessa, E. J. (2012). Reviving rehabilitation: The history, policies, and future of correctional reform. *Federal Probation, 76*(2), 47–56.

Lundahl, B. W., Kunz, C., Brownell, C., Tollefson, D., & Burke, B. L. (2010). A meta-analysis of motivational interviewing: Twenty-five years of empirical studies. *Research on Social Work Practice, 20*(2), 137–160.

Lurigio, A. J. (2001). *Drug treatment services for adult offenders: The state of the art*. National Institute of Justice.

Marlatt, G. A., & Donovan, D. M. (2005). *Relapse prevention: Maintenance strategies in the treatment of addictive behaviors* (2nd ed.). The Guilford Press.

McGuire, J. (2017). Cognitive-behavioural approaches to offenders: A review and prospects. *Current Opinion in Psychology, 13*, 54–59.

National Institute on Drug Abuse. (2020). *Genetics and substance abuse*. Retrieved from https://www.drugabuse.gov/publications/drugfacts/genetics-substance-abuse

Palmer, E., McGuire, J., & Kenney, R. (2017a). *From supervision to reintegration: Pathways and principles for effective offender reentry*. Routledge.

Palmer, E. J., McGuire, J., & Winder, B. (2017b). *Offender rehabilitation: From research to practice*. Routledge.

Peters, R., Murrin, M., & Ritter, A. (2020). Comorbid mental health and substance use disorders: A scoping review on treatment effectiveness. *Substance Abuse Treatment, Prevention, and Policy, 15*(1), 55. https://doi.org/10.1186/s13011-020-00294-4

Polaschek, D. L. L., Schmidt, S., Jordan, C.-E., Fiumara, D., & Doherty, S. (2020). The importance of identity change in prisoner reentry success: Findings from a multi-site randomized controlled trial. *Criminal Justice and Behavior, 47*(8), 892–911.

Sampson, R. J., Raudenbush, S. W., & Earls, F. (1997). Neighborhoods and violent crime: A multilevel study of collective efficacy. *Science, 277*(5328), 918–924. https://doi.org/10.1126/science.277.5328.918

Shapiro, F. (2018). *Eye movement desensitization and reprocessing (EMDR) therapy: Basic principles, protocols, and procedures*. Guilford Press.

Skeem, J. L., Manchak, S., & Peterson, J. K. (2016). Correctional policy for offenders with mental illness: Creating a new paradigm for recidivism reduction. *Law and Human Behavior, 40*(6), 604–616.

Teicher, M. H., Tomoda, A., & Andersen, S. L. (2006). Neurobiological consequences of early stress and childhood maltreatment: Are results from human and animal studies comparable? *Annals of the New York Academy of Sciences, 1071*(1), 313–323.

van der Kolk, B. (2005). Developmental trauma disorder: Toward a rational diagnosis for children with complex trauma histories. *Psychiatric Annals, 35*(5), 401–408.

Walsh, K., DiLillo, D., & Scalora, M. (2017). Trauma and cognitive distortions among incarcerated violent offenders: A moderating role for psychopathy. *Psychological Trauma: Theory, Research, Practice, and Policy, 9*(6), 727–734.

Widom, C. S. (1989). The cycle of violence. *Science, 244*(4901), 160–166.

Chapter 8
Concluding Chapter: The Power of Correctional Psychotherapy in Understanding Offending Populations

Understanding the characteristics of offending populations is fundamental for effective interventions and rehabilitation within the criminal justice system. In this concluding chapter, we bring together the main findings from this study to emphasize the significance of comprehending the unique characteristics of offenders. We also discuss contemporary issues prevalent in offender populations and explore the potential of correctional psychotherapy in advancing offender rehabilitation.

8.1 Factors Contributing to Criminal Behavior

Throughout the book, it became apparent that various factors contribute to the development and persistence of criminal behavior. These factors include social influences, such as family dynamics and peer associations, as well as psychological influences, such as mental health disorders and personality traits. Environmental influences, such as poverty and exposure to violence, also play a significant role. Understanding these factors is essential for the effective design and implementation of correctional psychotherapy programs.

8.1.1 Social Influences

Research has consistently shown that family dynamics, including dysfunctional relationships, neglect, and abuse, can significantly impact an individual's likelihood of engaging in criminal behavior. Additionally, peer associations, specifically involvement in delinquent peer groups, have been identified as a risk factor for criminal involvement. Correctional psychotherapy should address these social

K. Sapp, *Understanding Offending Populations and the Power of Correctional Psychotherapy*, SpringerBriefs in Offending Populations & Correctional Psychotherapy, https://doi.org/10.1007/978-3-031-45886-6_8

influences by providing support, guidance, and skill development to overcome negative social factors and establish positive relationships.

8.1.2 Psychological Influences

Psychological issues, such as substance abuse, mental health disorders, and cognitive deficits, are prevalent among offending populations. Correctional psychotherapy should prioritize addressing these underlying psychological issues to promote lasting behavioral change. Evidence-based therapeutic techniques, such as cognitive behavioral therapy (CBT), dialectical behavior therapy (DBT), and motivational interviewing, have shown promising results in mitigating psychological issues and reducing criminal behavior.

8.1.3 Environmental Influences

The environment in which individuals are raised and reside can significantly impact their likelihood of engaging in criminal behavior. Adverse neighborhood conditions, poverty, and exposure to violence have been identified as environmental factors that contribute to criminality. Correctional psychotherapy should consider the influence of these environmental factors and provide support in developing healthy coping strategies and creating positive environments for offenders.

8.2 Characteristics of Offending Populations

To effectively address the behavioral patterns of offending populations, it is essential to understand their characteristics. Offenders can present with diverse backgrounds, experiences, and risk factors. This section focuses on key characteristics that have been consistently identified in research as influential factors in criminal behavior.

8.2.1 Demographic Factors

Demographic factors, such as age, gender, and socioeconomic status, can significantly impact criminal behavior. For instance, studies have shown that young males from disadvantaged backgrounds are overrepresented in offender populations. Understanding these demographic factors helps tailor correctional psychotherapy to address the specific needs and challenges faced by different subsets of offenders.

8.2.2 *Criminogenic Needs*

Criminogenic needs refer to the underlying factors that contribute to criminal behavior. These needs can include substance abuse, poor impulse control, antisocial attitudes, lack of education or vocational skills, and limited problem-solving abilities. Correctional psychotherapy should be designed to target these criminogenic needs through evidence-based interventions that address each individual's unique risk factors.

8.3 Overview of Contemporary Issues in Offender Populations

The examination of contemporary issues in offender populations sheds light on the challenges facing correctional systems and the importance of addressing these issues through effective rehabilitation strategies. This section highlights some of the key contemporary issues prevalent in offender populations.

8.3.1 *Mental Health and Substance Abuse*

A significant proportion of the offending population struggle with mental health disorders and substance abuse issues. The co-occurrence of these conditions can complicate rehabilitation efforts and contribute to a higher risk of recidivism. Correctional psychotherapy must integrate mental health and substance abuse treatment to address the complex needs of these individuals adequately.

8.3.2 *Reintegration and Community Support*

Successful reintegration into the community is critical for reducing recidivism rates. Offenders face numerous challenges when transitioning back into society, such as securing employment, finding stable housing, and rebuilding relationships. Correctional psychotherapy should integrate strategies that focus on developing necessary life skills, fostering prosocial networks, and accessing community support systems.

8.4 Correctional Psychotherapy: Advancing Offender Rehabilitation

Correctional psychotherapy has the potential to play a transformative role in advancing offender rehabilitation. This section highlights the key components of correctional psychotherapy and discusses how it can be leveraged to promote positive change and reduce recidivism rates.

8.4.1 Evidence-Based Interventions

Correctional psychotherapy should employ evidence-based interventions, such as cognitive behavioral therapy (CBT), dialectical behavior therapy (DBT), and motivational interviewing. These interventions have demonstrated effectiveness in addressing criminogenic needs, promoting self-awareness and responsibility, and facilitating skill development for behavioral change.

8.4.2 Therapeutic Alliance and Engagement

Establishing a strong therapeutic alliance between therapists and offenders is crucial for effective correctional psychotherapy. Therapists need to foster a safe and supportive environment that encourages open communication, empathy, and trust. This approach enhances offender engagement in the therapeutic process and increases the likelihood of positive outcomes.

8.4.3 Multi-modal Approaches

Correctional psychotherapy should employ a multi-modal approach that addresses the diverse needs of individuals in offender populations. This includes incorporating individual therapy, group therapy, family therapy, and educational programs to create a comprehensive treatment framework that tackles various aspects of an offender's life.

8.5 Implications and Future Directions

The findings from this study have several implications for correctional practices and policies. First, it is crucial to prioritize investment in training, resources, and infrastructure to ensure the delivery of evidence-based correctional psychotherapy programs within correctional institutions. Second, collaboration between correctional systems, mental health professionals, and community support organizations is essential for successful rehabilitation and reintegration. Lastly, continued research is necessary to develop innovative and more effective therapeutic approaches that address the evolving needs of offending populations.

8.6 Conclusion

In conclusion, understanding the characteristics of offending populations and addressing contemporary issues are vital steps in advancing offender rehabilitation. Correctional psychotherapy holds great promise as a powerful tool in promoting positive change and reducing recidivism rates. By tailoring interventions to target criminogenic needs, employing evidence-based approaches, fostering strong therapeutic alliances, and adopting multi-modal frameworks, correctional psychotherapy can contribute significantly to the rehabilitation and successful reintegration of offenders. Continued research, collaboration, and innovation in this field are essential to refine existing approaches and develop new strategies for more effective offender rehabilitation.

Index

K. Sapp, *Understanding Offending Populations and the Power of Correctional Psychotherapy*, SpringerBriefs in Offending Populations & Correctional Psychotherapy , https://doi.org/10.1007/978-3-031-45886-6

www.ingramcontent.com/pod-product-compliance
Ingram Content Group UK Ltd.
Pitfield, Milton Keynes, MK11 3LW, UK
UKHW020150290926
15471UKWH00004B/783
* 9 7 8 3 0 3 1 4 5 8 8 5 9 *